Executive Presence:
Demonstrating Leadership in Times of Change and Uncertainty

– SARAH BRUMMITT –

D1407205

An environmentally friendly book printed and bound in England by
www.printondemand-worldwide.com

Mixed Sources
Product group from well-managed
forests, and other controlled sources
www.fsc.org Cert no. TT-COC-002641
© 1996 Forest Stewardship Council
FSC

PEFC
PEFC/16-33-415

PEFC Certified
This product is
from sustainably
managed forests
and controlled
sources
www.pefc.org

This book is made entirely of chain-of-custody materials

http://www.fast-print.net/bookshop

EXECUTIVE PRESENCE
Copyright © Sarah Brummitt 2015

A catalogue record for this book is available from the British Library

ISBN 978-178456-230-4

First published 2015 by
FASTPRINT PUBLISHING
Peterborough, England.

Foreword

I started my own leadership development business because I believe that professional men and women have an eye-watering amount of potential. My job is to help them unlock more of it and to support brilliant people in achieving whatever it is they want from their role and their career. This book would simply not be possible without my clients and it is to all of them that it is dedicated. I am also privileged to work with some amazingly talented, professional and patient associates, partners and suppliers – again, all of whom support my business through an array of skills and capabilities. To them I say a huge thank you. Finally, my heart belongs to wonderful friends who forever encourage and support what I do and of course, the 'Mortlake Massive' called 'B.A.S.H'.

"In these times of unprecedented change, your leadership and personal presence can be the only thing you rely on to help you deliver against your priorities. It is more important than ever that people are developing these skills faster, better, deeper"

Carrie Cushing, HR Director
GE Healthcare, UK & Ireland

"Another great book from this inspiring lady who made me realise the power of personal brand. Get ready for your next dose of Sarah Brummitt"

Donna Howden – Chair,
Telefónica UK Women's Network

"As a senior marketing leader in a small business, executive presence is essential. Our role as leaders is to galvanize our team to deliver in challenging times, and inspire them to create a customer experience that builds loyalty and revenue for our brand as well as our clients. Helping leaders develop the skills of influence, persuasion and impact is vital to commercial success. I have known and worked with Sarah Brummitt for a number of years and would certainly recommend her"

Rachel Swann, Commercial Director, Hive

"Sarah knows all the tips for success, even the little things you never thought would matter. From how one's clothes communicate different non-verbal messages, to how one's body language can betray or enhance one's verbal messages, you need only ask! She will not only tell you the answer, but she will give you examples, she will tell you why, and she will make it so real for you that you will not feel like you are sleepwalking into a career disaster ever again"

Lawyer, Financial Conduct Authority

"In our high-speed, technology focused age, it is arguably more important than ever to make the right impression - first time, every time. This is true for everyone, from senior leaders right down through an organization – and in the wider world beyond work. In this book, Sarah Brummitt provides practical tools and tips that everyone will benefit from"

Milica Gay, Financial Times Part Time Power Top 50, December 2013

Being able to stand out in today's connected and fast-paced business world requires an 'Executive Presence' and gravitas that commands attention. This is often a strong differentiator between those that we see succeed and those that tend to struggle in this new 'norm'

Andrew Williamson, Director, Ask-Teach Ltd

"Being coached by the outstanding Sarah Brummitt for the past 3 years has given me the courage to chase my ambitious dreams, she has taught me to be true to myself, have the courage to stand tall and believe in my capabilities as a leader and most importantly to celebrate my successes"

Louise Fellows, Board Director & Governor BCA College Maidenhead

Table of Contents

- The Survey Itself

CHAPTER THREE – WHAT IS EXECUTIVE PRESENCE?

- What the Research Revealed
- Confidence
- Charisma
- Poise
- Humility
- Credibility
- Authentic
- Self-awareness
- Life-long Learning
- Integrity
- What This All Means
- The Model for Executive Presence - LEADER

CHAPTER FOUR – THE LOOK OF A LEADER

- Why You Need to Care about Your 'Look'
- What We Asked and What the Research Revealed
- It's Instinctive
- Competence is a Given
- We All Have Expectations
- Science Supports the Psychology of Dressing
- Get It Right and We Notice You; Get It Wrong and We Notice the Clothes
- An American Example
- Our Friends in Greece
- We Also Get It Wrong in the UK

- And I'm Not Just Picking on the Men
- Remember, None of This is about Fashion
- We Don't all Have To Dress the Same
- All Facets of our Communication Have to 'Add Up'
- Even in Business we are Influenced by What's Going on Outside It
- The 'L' in LEADER Stands for 'Look'
- Avoiding the 'Yes, But' Game
- Getting the Look Right Consistently
- Evolve Your Visual Signature
- Deciding What's 'Appropriate'
- A Short Detour - the Backstory to 'Business Casual'
- So What *Is* Business Casual in the 21st Century?
- A Framework for Dressing
- Formality and our Choice of Clothing
  - The Messages behind a Suit
  - The Messages behind a Jacket
  - The Messages behind a Collar
  - The Messages behind no Collar
  - So What?
  - Fabric
  - Finish
  - Footwear
- Know What's Complementary: Fit, Fit, Fit, Fit, Fit
- The Reality That We All Just Have To Get Used To
- Men and Women and Shapes
- Wearing the Right Colour
- Complete Immaculate Grooming

- Pay Attention to Detail
- Signing off on Image

CHAPTER FIVE – ENGAGE LIKE A LEADER

- What is meant by 'Engage'?
- What The Research Revealed
- Why is Integrity so Important to Convey for Leaders who have Executive Presence?
- How does a Leader 'Do' Integrity?
- How does a Leader *Communicate* Purpose?
- How does a Leader 'Do' Authenticity?
- How does a Leader *Communicate* Vulnerability?
- How does a Leader 'Do' Respect?
- How does a Leader 'Do' Humility?
- How does a Leader 'Do' Poise?
- How does a Leader 'Do' Confidence?
- How does a Leader 'Do' Credibility?
- How does a Leader 'Do' Self-Awareness?
- How does a Leader Win Hearts and Minds?
- How does a Leader Challenge and Support Their People?

CHAPTER SIX – ACT LIKE A LEADER

- What is Meant By 'Act'?
- What We Asked
- What the Research Revealed
- Different Perspectives Depending on Role Level
- Listening and Leadership
- Listening Louder

- Level 1 – Cosmetic Listening (In Other Words, I'm Not Listening)
- Level 2 – Conversational Listening (Sorry, I Am Still Not Listening)
- Level 3 – Active Listening (Hurrah, I Am Listening – A Bit)
- Level 4 – Exquisite Listening (Wow, I Am Right in the Zone)
- The Importance of Non-Verbal Communication
- Misquoting Mehrabian
- De-coding Body Language
- Making our Non Verbal Communication Work For and Not Against Us
  - Handshake Heaven or Hell?
  - Handshakes to Avoid if You Want to Convey Presence
  - Making Your Handshake Count
  - Eye Contact
  - Head Up
  - To Nod or Not To Nod?
  - Walk Tall
  - Our Hands Reveal Our Inner Thoughts
  - Make them Visible
  - Use them for Emphasis not Exaggeration
  - Learn to Steeple
  - Thumbs Up and Out
  - Batoning
  - Deliberate, Measured, Movements for Emphasis
  - Avoid Certain Gestures that can Offend
  - Preening
  - Fiddling and Twiddling

- Evolving as a Leader

CHAPTER NINE – RESONATE LIKE A LEADER

- What is meant by Resonate?
- What We Asked
- What the Research Revealed
- Clear, Concise Communication
- Being Persuasive with Language
- Why Storytelling?
- Three Different Types of Story
- Building a Great Story
- Narrative Structures
- What all Good Stories also have
    o A Clear Objective
    o Attention Grabbers
    o Give me some Context
    o Metaphor and Analogy Turn Tedious, Dry, Boring Topics into
    o Repeatable Sound Bites
- The Telling of a Great Story
    o Lower, Slower, Clearer
    o The Power of the Pause
    o High Rising Terminals (HRT)
    o Fillers - Otherwise Known as the 'Sentence Stuffer' or a 'Rubbish' Word
    o Knowing when to Stop Talking
    o Be Brief, Be Brilliant and Be Done
    o Avoid Sharing Internal Dialogue
- Language that Resonates

- State Things that People want to Agree With
- Use 'Our', 'We' and 'Us' rather than 'You', 'I' and 'Me'
- Because, Because, Because, Because
- Affirmative Language
- Assertive Language
- Things Great Leaders Never Say
- Things Great Leaders Always Say
- It's Time to Talk about the 'F' Word
- How to Give Good Feedback
- Chairmanship Skills
- Making Suggestions (for Content or Procedure)
- Building
- Supporting
- Signposting
- Bringing in/Shutting out
- Testing Understanding
- Summarizing
- The Cross Cultural Context
- What People Say and What They Actually Mean

Bibliography

Introduction

This book has been written in a way that offers you choice. If you wish, you can 'dip in and out' of different chapters that hold the most fascination, relevance and interest to you personally as you consider how you convey 'Executive Presence' and demonstrate leadership in times of change and uncertainty. Alternatively, you can start at the beginning and finish at the end. Every chapter has been structured in a way to provide information, resources, tips and stories and weaved throughout it is a 'so, how do I do more of that?' practical approach. *For each and every chapter* I could have written another 20,000 words - easily. However, I also recognize the challenge facing all leaders – time. You have a 'day job' and there are many different, brilliant, insightful resources that you could also read (many of which are referenced in this book). I also appreciate that there may be other areas of your professional development on which you may wish to focus. Hence, I have made choices. There is always more to say and no time in which to say it, however please do feel free to contact me directly with your questions, comments and enquiries. I would be delighted to help.

Sarah Brummitt
June 2015

Chapter One –
The Necessity of This
Conversation

*"The definition of a leader is someone whom people
will follow. That means connecting with your
colleagues more powerfully than ever before"*

Sarah Brummitt - 2012

In 2007 I was asked to meet with a high potential
talent in a FTSE 500 business, with a view to
supporting him with some executive coaching. Let's
for the sake of argument call him Roy. Roy had a first
class degree, a MA and a MBA. Quite how he
managed all of that with a young family I don't know,
but this was clearly an extremely bright, capable,
hardworking man. He worked in the IT part of the
value chain and let's just say that he worked in the
finance sector. Roy was an ambitious person,
relatively young and someone who had been asked to
meet me after being unsuccessful with an internal,
high profile promotion opportunity that had come up
within his business. As a successful professional, and
in addition to being extraordinarily bright, Roy was
extremely conscientious, demonstrated superb

attention to detail and was highly organized. Roy was renowned for being fast to act in relation to IT challenges that the business posed to him and his team. So, what was the problem? Why wasn't Roy getting on and getting ahead in the way that he wanted? Quite simply the challenge for Roy had nothing to do with his technical ability. His expertise in this area was beyond repute. In essence the challenge for Roy represented the joke about doctors who become fascinated by the disease but couldn't care less about the patient. In other words, he had become overly focused on the technical nature of his profession and lost sight of the essentially relationship nature of his role. He was a leader in a relationship business that just happened to be in a very successful global organization. Roy had not understood the need to focus on the skills behind building collaborative, effective and successful relationships all around his business because he was overly reliant on his domain strength being sufficient. It wasn't. In essence, Roy lacked 'Executive Presence'.

So let's start with some definitions. The word 'executive' is as good a place as any to begin. For those of you reading this who are already thinking 'well, I'm not an executive so this doesn't apply to me', just stop for a second. Change the word 'executive' to 'leadership' and you are in the game. Now those of you thinking 'well, I'm not really a leader', then let me stop you there. You don't need direct reports and job titles to be a leader. Everyone who needs to influence others is a leader. However, if you don't like that word, change 'leader' to 'professional' and then you too are in this club. I did have one person say to me 'I'm not a professional in the traditional sense' (and no, I don't know why *anyone would think that* but bear with me), you too can just stop right there. Anyone doing a job for which they are paid would *want* be described as professional, wouldn't they? Even so, if you can't bear that word, then change it to 'personal' and you too are joining this party.

Here is the point: if you have any kind of role, responsibility, requirement or just plain old appetite to persuade, engage, inform, involve, inspire, motivate, coach, counsel, support, encourage, develop, collaborate, manage, lead, sell, advise, consult, direct, mentor, teach, train, guide, belong or communicate with other people, then you need this book. Why? This book is all about demonstrating influence and the skills and strategies to do so exquisitely, effectively, authentically, consistently, intentionally and successfully.

And here's something else. What I've noticed over the last few years is just how many people I know (both professionally and personally) who truly struggle with this. Please don't misunderstand my point, as I don't mean to sound rude. I've had the privilege and the pleasure of working with, and for, an enormous array of bright, talented, capable, intelligent, decent, successful people. However, if you're thinking 'yep,

I'm like them, I'm rather fabulous even if I do say so myself and I think I'm able to do all of this already' then all I can say is again, just wait a moment. Yes, if it's friends, loved ones, sycophants with a vested interest in thinking you're marvelous, trusted colleagues, people who are just like us, then all of those people do not count. It's when you find yourself with people, in places, whom you don't know, who don't care about you and who may not even like you…that's *especially* when you need 'presence'. If you're trying to get on, get ahead, get past an issue – whether it's with people you like or people you don't and who may not give a rip about what you're trying to do…that's when you need presence. When you're trying to drive something forward, make progress; achieve something…that's when you need 'presence'. When you're bored, hungry, angry, tired and/or depressed and you *still* need to influence others…that's when you need 'presence'. When you'd rather curl up and die, or at least curl up and drink rather than do what you have to do…that's when you need 'presence'.

Everything I've just written in the previous paragraph is my own personal experience and consequent belief in the necessity of this conversation. It's based on 25 years in corporate life in one form or another, and yet even so, let us assume for a minute that none of what I have said is true. What else can we turn to in order to validate the need for the conversation? Why should you 'buy' any of this? Well, settle back and listen up because there is a boatload of other – empirically robust - reasons to pay attention to this topic as a leader, a professional and an influencer of others.

Globalization

The way businesses do business has completely changed. Let's start by talking about globalization (why not? I hear you say). Businesses today operate in a global market that has driven greater competition and convergence. What do I mean? As more of a business's products and services are consumed outside of its home nation, what we want starts to become more similar around the world. Think for a moment about Starbucks, McDonalds or Apple just by way of example. Go into any of their stores, restaurants or coffee shops anywhere in the world and their aim is for you to have an absolutely consistent consumer experience – no matter where you are. We now live in a world where organizations are more global and more cross-cultural than ever before. The phrase 'global village' is littered all over the place. When you consider the challenge of working across borders, communicating across cultures, understanding the nuances of different languages, scheduling meetings across time zones and doing all of the above at a distance. Nowadays we may rarely (if ever), be in the same place as our colleagues, our boss or our team. Quite simply this is the new norm of business and by God do we need to be able to convey presence and influence if we're going to survive, thrive and succeed at it.

Flatter Structures

The professional world of business has never been more fluid. It used to be the case in the not so distant past that there were two kinds of companies – those going through change – and those remaining static. Organizations today exist in an environment of continual change. New bosses, new teams, new structures, new relationships, new roles and new responsibilities – all of which require an ability to engage, influence and deliver. By the way – the Harvard Business Review[156] would argue that up to 70% of those change initiatives fail. So, if it wasn't enough to have to be exquisitely influential amid all that change; leaders today also then need to be equipped with the influencing skill set to deal with the fallout from the vast majority of all that change failing to deliver the expected results.

The shape of business today has been transformed. In the UK, with a handful of exceptions (the health service, law firms, the armed forces and the civil service), organizations are now much flatter. Why? Because the sheer necessity of survival in a competitive landscape means that companies which can be more responsive, leaner and faster to execute stand the best chance of surviving. By flattening hierarchies and structures, businesses can make decisions more quickly because there are fewer levels of management and we are closer to the key decision makers than ever before. That has enormous ramifications in terms of professionals and their ability to stand out. Quite simply, this requires us to be much more influential and impactful.

Still not persuaded? Okay, let's keep going.

Matrix Organizations are the Norm

Not only are businesses 'flatter', but also the connections between and within businesses have changed. Flatter organizations tend to encourage more horizontal networks and ways of working. Professionals now live in what is widely known as a 'matrix organization' where the challenge is to engage, persuade, influence and motivate people who don't fit into the traditional model of organizational hierarchy. These people don't *have* to do anything for us...and yet we need them to. We cannot make them, direct them, instruct them, force them, coerce them, blackmail them or bully them to support our plan – we *have to effectively* influence them.

We Live in a New Leadership Paradigm

McKinsey published a report in January 2015[54] which reinforces the new leadership realities for organizations across the world. Those are uncertainty, ambiguity, chaos and change. Wow! Leadership against this backdrop has simply never been so challenging. In our recent history the global financial crisis of 2007-2008 is considered by many economists to be the worst financial firestorm since the crash and subsequent depression of the 1930s. In the US, almost 18% of households have been under what economists term 'financial distress' as a result of the crisis and that number remains steady. A similar pattern (and in some countries a much more pronounced one) has emerged in Europe with people owing more, owning less and enduring significant changes in lifestyle. What's that got to do with presence I hear you ask? Well, simply this – our outlook, our mindset, our morale and our levels of engagement have been severely and sorely tested. You try motivating a technician in a body shop who's living on a minimum wage with an effective year-on-year drop in living standards. It's not easy.

But don't just take my word for it.

McKinsey's[54] article had a simple premise: 'Decoding leadership: what really matters?' Over 189,000 people were surveyed across 81 organizations, in a global context. The premise was to explore specific leadership behaviours that were most frequently applied to drive performance. A 'top 20' was compiled and from that, four specific kinds of behavior drove 89% of leadership effectiveness. Number 1 was 'be supportive', followed by 'operate with a strong results orientation', 'seek different perspectives' and 'solve problems effectively'. All four of those traits sit within the model of 'Executive Presence' and I would strongly argue that at least two of those require a set of influencing skills like no other.

The 'Born Leader' Mantra is Dead

There is a myth around leadership and of leaders who are successful. That myth says that we have to be extraordinary people; we have to be magical, mystical, amazing and extraordinary. We perpetuate that myth with the 'born leader' analogy. For far too long, we have believed that leadership was this super special gift that only some of us were lucky enough to have. Leadership isn't about exceptional people at all. It's about ordinary people who act and speak in an extraordinary and very different way. What they do and how they do it – well, read on. Leaders today need to inspire, engage, motivate, delight, collaborate with and enthuse our teams, colleagues, shareholders, suppliers and customers is a level of exquisite influence like never before. Sound difficult? It is. If you don't believe me, feel free to browse through an organization's employee engagement survey. Even those (not the majority) who are getting right; recognize that there's no opportunity to rest on your laurels.

Our People Have Never Been More Different

Fortunately, and not before time, workforces don't look, sound or behave in a homogenous fashion. Even though we still have an eye-watering distance still to go to achieve anything like parity (or something that even vaguely reflects the society in which we live), businesses today are far more diverse. We're not all white men of a certain age and socio-economic background (and I say that with - sincerely – not a shred of disrespect to white men of a certain age and socio-economic background). One set of rules and norms are no longer *the* set of rules and norms.

Here are a few diversity facts about the UK in 2015[157]. Ethnic minority and cultural groups account for 8% of the UK population. Asian or Asian British = 50%, Black or Black British = 25%, Mixed Race = 15%, Chinese = 5%, Other = 5%. Among UK nationals, 6.1% are from a black or minority ethnic (BME) background. This compares with 8.7% in the UK employed population. Among all academic staff, including international staff, the black or minority ethnic [BME] percentage is higher at 10.9%.

Our Working Lives are Longer

What else can I tell the sceptics amongst you? Ah, yes – let's talk about the impact of working longer than any workforce generation before us. In the United Kingdom we're working longer than ever before with a predicted average retirement age that is continuing to rise. Those young people born in 1993 will be unlikely to be able to retire before the age of 70. Indeed, while we're at it, let's examine some facts in relation to multi-generational workforces. In the UK there are "Stabilizing" Traditionalists, born prior to 1946, "transformational" Baby Boomers, born between 1946 and 1964, "entrepreneurial" Generation X, born between 1965 and 1980 and "always on" Millennials, sometimes called Generation Y, born between 1981 and 2000. Our colleagues, co-workers and friends at the office are now old enough to be *our grandchildren*. The generation gap has taken on a never-seen-before expanse that we're only just starting to comprehend. How 'on earth' do you engage as a 'baby boomer' with a 'digital native'? (And for those of you currently thinking 'what is she talking about?' then I rest my case.) So, if we are going to get on with these people, never mind be able to collaborate, communicate and co-operate effectively with them, then we will need behavioural flexibility the likes of which we've never seen before.

Do you need more? Are you *still* sat there thinking 'yes but despite all that I am the most brilliant (insert the name of whichever profession you like) there has ever been?' I'm only half tongue-in-cheek when I pose the question. Well, okay then…let's play along and say 'so you are, well done…now sit down and keep reading' – because here's why, despite *all of the above* not relating to you and your influencing skills; then here are the stark, simple facts.

We Don't Think Like We Used To

Dan Levitin's book *'The Organized Mind'*[36] is an excellent read and lays the facts bare. In a nutshell, his premise is that it's never been as important as it is now to 'pay attention to how we pay attention'. The fact is that we are being bombarded with information that simply wasn't in existence before now.

The statistics reveal that human beings now take in the equivalent of 175 newspapers worth of information every single day. If I put it another way, we take onboard five times more information than we did in 1986 every single day. All of us now live in a world with 300 hexabytes of human-made information (apparently that's 300 with 18 zeros after it). Google estimated that there was only 30 hexabytes in existence only a few years ago; so we have been busy creating more information than previously existed in the whole of human history before now.

So what?

We Don't Listen Like We Used To

We've never been so overwhelmed, absorbed, distracted and confused by all this data. Our brain is just eye-wateringly busy trying to process, store, recall, redistribute, utilize and prioritize *more information than the whole of human history before now. Add to that all of the things that I've just outlined that somehow we all have to cope with.* And then along comes your good self – armed with that devilish 'I do it my way' kind of professionalism. You bring with you intelligence, for sure; wit and skill, no doubt; a decent person, of course, but also you offer (on occasion) an ineffective way of conveying impact, presence and influence to boot. You're terribly sorry, but it will be worth it for the rest of us to look past the shambles, decipher the ambiguity, and stick with you whilst you ramble incessantly off the point. It's down to us to work out, get past and get over all the things that are getting in the way of understanding *precisely* what on earth you are talking about and why on earth we should care about it.

In other words, *you want us to do all the work for you.* Well quite simply, you can forget it. It would have been an enormous ask if the rest of our world had been relatively stable, but given that the last almost four pages has also laid out what else has been going on, then you can quite understand that we are all terribly sorry but we're actually very, very, very busy with this other entire nonsense mate, to work out what you're all about. It's much quicker not to bother. So believe me, we don't.

Our Technical Capability is Assumed

Why does every leader need to demonstrate Executive Presence? Why not just focus on being an outstanding technical contributor? Won't we succeed if we focus on demonstrating brilliant domain strength in our area of expertise and know that that will do it? Quite simply, no it won't. If only it were that simple. For the early part of our career it makes complete sense to focus on our domain strength. In other words, if I want to be a marketer, I should do all the training, get all the support and experience to become a good marketer. I should take as many additional qualifications as I can, broaden my knowledge and become technically superb. And yet. If that's *all* I focus on doing, then there is no doubt (much like Roy at the top of this chapter), that I will become frustrated.

Empirical Evidence Backs Up the Need for 'Executive Presence'

This book is based on qualitative and quantitative research that I commissioned a survey expert to complete. One of the questions that the audience was asked was 'do you agree that Executive Presence is a vital component of being a leader?' Options from which to choose to answer this question were simply 'yes', 'no' or 'don't know'. 91% of the survey respondents said 'yes' to this question. In addition, survey respondents were then asked 'do you believe that Executive Presence can be developed?' Again, 91% said 'yes', 5% said 'I'm not sure' and 4% said 'no'. The point of introducing some of the survey results so early is simply this: leaders see this quality as overwhelmingly important for a leader to possess, plus it is seen as something which is possible to evolve, develop, enhance, shape, and improve in terms of our effectiveness.

Great Minds Support the Argument

Peter Drucker[134] is one of the most brilliant management thinkers of our age, and he is certainly one of the most extensively published. One of my favourite quotes from him is simply this: 'only three things happen naturally in organizations: friction, confusion, and underperformance. Everything else requires leadership"[73]. Quite simply, that's true, and if we're going to navigate through that and pull people along with us then that will require a set of influencing skills like no other. Malcolm Gladwell commented in his brilliant book 'Blink'[110] that: "the difference between generating resistance and enthusiasm is narrower than we imagine". Well said sir! Generating enthusiasm requires presence; a lack of it will generate resistance. And there are many more besides.

The case for the necessity of this conversation is now made. If, dear reader, you still believe that this topic might not matter to you, your colleagues, your teams, your customers, your suppliers and your organizations, then all I can say is 'good luck' to you. Everyone needs to consider how he or she conveys Executive Presence because it's the hallmark of all great leaders. It's how you *demonstrate* leadership in times of change and uncertainty, and succeed against the backdrop of everything that has just been laid out over the last few pages. How *do you* communicate leadership to people in a way that inspires and engages them to consistently, enthusiastically and continually deliver? How *do you* influence *exquisitely?* This book will combine a vast array of practical strategies from which to pick and choose, robust empirical data to support the argument and a generous smattering of real-life stories to lead the way.

Chapter Two –
The Structure of The Survey

"There are lies, damn lies and statistics"
Benjamin Disraeli

For this research to have credibility I knew that (a) I wasn't to design or conduct it myself and (b) I needed to get professional help. So I did – in the form of a qualitative and quantitative research expert who scoped the remit for the research and helped shift and shape the people who were to be targeted. This chapter is designed to explain the structure, responses and key findings from the survey.

Demographics of Respondents

Let me tell a little about the people who responded to my survey:

- 57% were male
- 43% were female
- The age profile revealed categories ranging from under 21 to 65 and over
- For male respondents, the biggest proportion was in the 45-54 age range

- For female respondents, the biggest proportion was in the 35-44 age range

Industries Represented

We asked respondents which industry sector they represented and the range covered:

- Advertising/PR
- Banking/Finance
- Education
- Healthcare
- IT/Internet
- Legal
- Media/Creative
- Consultancy
- Property
- Telecommunications
- Travel/Transport

The largest sector represented in the survey came from the consultancy arena, however, for the free form section of the survey there was little difference between the amount of responses between the consultancy and corporate sectors.

Functional Profile of Respondents

What parts of the value chain did the respondents to my survey represent? Specifically:

- Communications
- Customer Service
- Design
- Finance
- Human Resources
- Marketing
- Operations
- Organization Development
- Production
- Sales/Business Development
- Strategy

Perhaps not surprisingly there were some biases that were revealed (and can't be controlled). For example, there were a statistically significantly higher proportion of females in Human Resources, and the Sales/Business Development function represented 30% of the total number of respondents.

Hierarchical Profile of Respondents

This is really answering the question regarding the level of seniority within an organization represented by respondents, who self-selected. Specifically:

- Business Owner
- Board Level Executive
- Senior Manager
- Middle Manager

- Front Line Manager
- Specialist
- Team Member

Again, a gender distinction revealed itself. Outside of business owners (for which not surprisingly both men and women were represented), in the corporate environment the most senior female respondent was a Senior Manager. The next most senior female respondent was a team member. Compare this to male respondents where the two board level executives were male and the next most senior role represented by men was senior manager. You get the point. Men who responded were in more senior roles and this was a statistically significant distinction.

The Survey Itself
The Look of Executive Presence

We form impressions quickly and initially based on visual information. To answer the following questions, consider someone who conveys a strong Executive Presence through their appearance in your organization.

How important is a Leader's image and appearance to your perception of them professionally?

We asked the following questions to which respondents answered across the following scale:

- *Extremely important*
- *Important*
- *Moderately important*
- *Slightly important*
- *Not important at all*

When you think of a leader with Executive Presence, how much do you think the following factors influence your perception of their credibility?

- *If they have good looks*
- *If they are tall*
- *If they walk with confidence*
- *If they use gestures to reinforce points*
- *If they have good general health*
- *If they are physically fit*
- *If they have good posture*

We asked the following questions to which respondents answered across the following scale:

- *Extremely important*
- *Important*
- *Moderately important*

- *Slightly important*
- *Not important at all*

How important are these other factors in projecting a strong Executive Presence?

- *Quality clothing*
- *Sharp tailoring*
- *Wearing a tie (gentlemen)*
- *Wearing a jacket*
- *Wearing a skirt or dress (ladies)*
- *Wearing bold colours/style*
- *Showing attention to detail in appearance*
- *Wearing current fashion*
- *Expensive clothing accessories (i.e. shoes, watch, jewelry)*
- *High quality business accessories (i.e. briefcase or bag, laptop, mobile, phone, pen)*
- *Immaculate grooming*

We asked the following questions to which respondents answered across the following scale:

- *Extremely important*
- *Important*
- *Moderately important*
- *Slightly important*
- *Not important at all*

The Personal Characteristics behind Executive Presence

These questions are designed to explore what personal characteristics and values underpin Executive Presence.

Please select the top three characteristics that you believe makes a leader most compelling. Audience selected 'most important', 'second' and 'third':

- *Ambition*
- *Good humour*
- *Authenticity*
- *Integrity*
- *Compassion*
- *Recognition*
- *Loyalty*
- *Power*
- *Respect*
- *Creativity*
- *Humanity*
- *Vulnerability*
- *Competitiveness*
- *Harmony*

How important do you think these personal characteristics are in connecting leaders with those they lead?

- *Extremely important*
- *Important*
- *Moderately important*
- *Slightly important*
- *Not important at all*

The Behaviours Demonstrative Of Executive Presence

This section aims to draw out your views on how successful leaders behave.

The narrative structure for answering the following questions was as follows:

- *Strongly agree*
- *Agree*
- *Neither agree nor disagree*
- *Slightly disagree*
- *Strongly disagree*

Please indicate the extent to which you believe successful leaders demonstrate the following behaviours:

- *They have clear, concise communication*
- *They use positive body language (e.g. smile, nod)*
- *They maintain good eye contact*

- *They use gestures highly effectively*
- *They appear in control at all times*
- *They put others at ease*
- *They listen*
- *They reassure*
- *They admit when they are wrong*
- *They always focus on the positive, even when things are going wrong*

Which one of these behaviours is the single most important in your view for being successful as a leader?

- *They have clear, concise communication*
- *They use positive body language (e.g. smile, nod)*
- *They maintain good eye contact*
- *They use gestures highly effectively*
- *They appear in control at all times*
- *They put others at ease*
- *They listen*
- *They reassure*
- *They admit when they are wrong*
- *They always focus on the positive, even when things are going wrong*

The Decisions which Demonstrate Executive Presence

This section aims to understand your views on how Leaders made effective decisions.

The narrative structure for answering the following questions was as follows:

- *Strongly agree*
- *Agree*
- *Neither agree nor disagree*
- *Slightly disagree*
- *Strongly disagree*

In crisis situations, people with Executive Presence make decisions that are:

- *Well considered*
- *Based on extensive research*
- *Made quickly*
- *Based on consultation*
- *Consistently applied*
- *Communicated clearly*
- *Based on facts*
- *Based on intuition*
- *Based on a combination of facts and intuition*

In times of uncertainty, people with Executive Presence make decisions that are:

- *Well considered*
- *Based on extensive research*
- *Made quickly*
- *Based on consultation*
- *Consistently applied*
- *Communicated clearly*
- *Based on facts*
- *Based on intuition*
- *Based on a combination of facts and intuition*

In making important decisions about their company's future, people with Executive Presence make decisions that are:

- *Well considered*
- *Based on extensive research*
- *Made quickly*
- *Based on consultation*
- *Consistently applied*
- *Communicated clearly*
- *Based on facts*
- *Based on intuition*
- *Based on a combination of facts and intuition*

In making decisions that affect others' lives, people with Executive Presence make decisions that are:

- *Well considered*
- *Based on extensive research*
- *Made quickly*
- *Based on consultation*
- *Consistently applied*
- *Communicated clearly*
- *Based on facts*
- *Based on intuition*
- *Based on a combination of facts and intuition*

The Communication of Executive Presence

This final section examines your views on how people with Executive Presence communicate.

When speaking, the most effective leader I know does:

- *Pace*
- *Pitch*
- *Structure*
- *Variation in tone*
- *Emphasis*

When speaking, the least effective leader I know does:

- *Pace*
- *Pitch*
- *Structure*
- *Variation in tone*
- *Emphasis*

What three things make a leader's message most compelling (indicate in order of priority)? The narrative structure for answering this question is 'most compelling', 'second' and 'third'.

- *Challenging message*
- *Passion*
- *Presented an exciting vision of the future*
- *Very relevant to the audience*
- *Interesting story*
- *Clarity of points communicated*
- *Honest appraisal of how difficult it will be to achieve*
- *Very open explanation of rationale for decision*
- *Use of visuals*
- *Tailored message to the audience*

Defining Executive Presence

Executive Presence describes a complex set of elements required to be credible as a leader. This section aims to explore views on what Executive Presence is.

Put these factors into the order of their importance for being an effective leader, where 1 is the most important and 5 is the least important:

- *How a leader looks*
- *How a leader connects with those they are leading*
- *How a leader behaves*
- *How a leader thinks and makes decisions*
- *How a leader verbally communicates*

What else would you consider to be important in having Executive Presence? (This was a free form text box).

Do you agree that Executive Presence is a vital component of being a leader?

- *Yes*
- *No*
- *I'm not sure*

Do you believe that Executive Presence can be developed?

- *Yes*
- *No*
- *I'm not sure*

If you were to define Executive Presence now, what words or phrases come to mind as you think of someone who you believe has it? (This was a free form text box).

Chapter Three –
What Is Executive Presence?

*"The difference between generating resistance and
enthusiasm is narrower than we imagine"*

Malcolm Gladwell

I commissioned a professional qualitative and
quantitative research professional to conduct a survey
to understand the definition, components and key
considerations around 'Executive Presence'. It's a
phrase I've heard a number of times and in a number
of different contexts, however, there was no clarity
with regard to what it actually means. It certainly
sounded great and who wouldn't want to be described
in those terms as a Leader. So, I was simply curious to
understand what exactly the phrase 'Executive
Presence' means.

What the Research Revealed

We asked:

If you were to define Executive Presence now, what words or phrases come to mind to describe someone who you believe has it?

Below is a random selection of form response responses to this question:

Responses	Age Range	Free Form Response
Board Level Executives	35-44	Inspirational, unshockable, calm.
	45-54	Confident, articulate, charismatic, leads by example, polished, well groomed. The ability to motivate self and others and handle adversity.
Business Owners	35-44	Honest and open relationship with the leadership team. People skills – understanding the values

		and beliefs of individuals.
		Authenticity, integrity, clarity and conviction in thought and communication.
		A person who demonstrates gravitas, experience and integrity. Looks good in their physic and their dress at all times, and relates to those around him/her by listening and giving clear communication of direction and vision.
	45-54	High level of integrity, open and honest, relevant, highly informed, challenging, engaging, business focused, people focused, balanced.
		The ability to connect and engage, confidence, competence, humility, integrity, ability to communicate, intelligence,

		intuition, commitment, respect, honesty, trust, consistency, professional or appropriate image for role/stakeholders/ customers/colleagues, appropriate humour, passion.
		Magnetic, inspiring, sexy, though provoking, intellectual, original, dynamic, brave, flexible.
		Passionate and visionary.
		Professional, gravitas, polished, authenticity.
		The person is authentic and thoughtful. They are trusted. He/she makes decisions carefully weighing up the evidence and consulting others. This individual will also draw on their own experience and use their intuition in making a decision. This

		decision will be carefully and clearly communicated to different audiences in ways that are appropriate for each one. They will then follow through on what needs to be done. When things go wrong the individual will acknowledge this and search to understand the reasons. This does not mean apportioning blame but seeking to work out the best way to achieve the required outcome and not make the same or further mistakes. When success is realized, a leader will celebrate success and will acknowledge others achievements. Great strong presence, intelligent, connects with people well, considers much before acting, and is authentic and real. Role model, visionary,

		human, shows emotion.
		Compelling, confident, assured, knowledgeable, groomed, attention to detail, empathetic.
	55-64	Honesty, integrity and for people to wholeheartedly believe in what they say and do.
		Integrity, flexibility, clarity, self-responsibility, vision, coherence. Charisma and a social conscience. Empathy
		Track record of success.
	65+	It must be presence in the right context. In other words, if you are in a fashion creative company, fashion is important. If you are in a bank, fashion is almost always detrimental.

		Context and nuance is key.
	65+	Appropriate to the culture of the business.
Senior Manager	26-34	Knowledge, skill, integrity, respected by peers/colleagues, ability to empathize, good communication skills, self-control, dressed to suit their own professional style.
	35-44	Gravitas, authenticity, knowledge, trusted, creativity, problem solving Polished and fluent in verbal communication skills. Inquiring. Passion. Ability to connect with people.

		Listen. Have vision. Makes decisions. Accountable, inspiring. A person who has the ability to influence others by being perceptive and understanding. This person would be compassionate, humble and have charisma. Calm/collected, measured, educated/in possession of all relevant facts, honest. Self-awareness, self-confidence, empathy.
	45-54	Presence – makes an impact as soon as they walk into a room. Self-confident. Openly friendly and approachable. Good listener. Positive responses.
Middle Manager	26-34	Sleek, never puts a foot wrong, controlled, makes you feel 'safe' in their presence, gets people to open up.

	35-44	Always looks well put together. Communicates effectively. Uses experience and information to make decisions.
Front-line Manager	35-44	Feedback, positive or negative can be a great motivation whether the job is large or small.
	45-54	Positive and broaden the horizon attitude. Respectful.
Specialist	26-34	Always very calm even when he doesn't have the answers, he will explore questions with people, never in a flap, dependable, never appears to doubt himself but in a calm collected way, not an overbearing arrogant way.
	45-54	Leadership. Honesty. Integrity. Communication.

		Humour. Perspective. Credibility. Rational. Positive. Realistic. Honest. Compelling. Charismatic. Inspirational.
Team Member	Under 21	Good personality, outgoing, down to earth, easy to relate to, very passionate, very good knowledge and understanding.
	26-34	Deep respect for others. Empowering others. Integrity. Leading by example. Consistency. Honesty.
	35-44	Credibility, confidence, competence, inspirational, risk taker, intelligent, strategist, courageous, insightful, empathetic, genuine, honest, determined, effective communicator, engaging self-awareness, image conscious, sociable and

		warm.
	45-54	Personable, human, beguiling, believable, amazing. Charisma, stature. This is someone who is believable but touchable in the complete sense of the word, someone who you feel hears what you say.
Male Responses	**Age Range**	**Free Form Response**
Board Level Execs	45-54	Strong, reassuring, calm, thoughtful, action-oriented. Confident, charismatic, considered and creative. You would pitch them in any debate on business if they were a business leader.

| Business Owners | 35-44 | Gravitas. Integrity. Authenticity. Modesty. Lack of ego. Unswerving commitment to achieving the goal. Knowing what they don't know. Ability to trust others. Clarity of their role in empowering others to succeed 'it's not about them'. Someone who inspires me to think, dream and do the seemingly impossible. Dynamic, well rounded, balanced. Honest, open, trusting, considerate, fair, well groomed, measured, consistent. Lose the ego. |
| | 45-54 | Impact defined by 'believability'. Curiosity. Passionate listener who can respond with authority and credibility.

The individual must be confident, assertive. Has the ability to make difficult decisions, with the backbone to see those decisions to their |

		conclusion. Must be a good communicator and have the ability to connect with people and be able to motivate them.

Stature, power, respect, innovative, creative, dynamic.

Personal power, presence, insightful, clear communicator, approachable, authentic. Considered but decisive. Energetic but still. "Leadership is a matter of intelligence, trustworthiness, humaneness, courage and sternness".

Sun Tzu said "tough but kind, straightforward yet cunning". Xenophon. "To win without fighting is best".

Clear communicator, |

		emotional intelligence, passion, respect, integrity, honesty, time, energy.
	55-64	Honesty, compassion.
		Ability to motivate those around them.
		Having a great professional profile.
		Groundedness.
		Honesty, consistency and transparency.
Senior Managers	26-34	Attention to individual team members.
	35-44	Experience, presence, drive, ambition. Drive, direction and goals.
	45-54	Somebody who is

		passionate and who is driven. Respect, knowledge, trustworthiness, gravitas, empathy, credibility, gravitas, stature, personality with humor, articulate, Knowledgeable, passion, challenging and empathy. Intelligence and understanding. Gravitas, empathy and credibility. They have gravitas – it's hard to qualify the make-up of this but for example, Gordon Brown vs. Bill Clinton.
	55-64	Clarity of vision, clear communication, Consistent. Having the right team and advisors around you. Being grounded in reality and having credibility.

		Brainpower, people skills and strategy and vision are vital. Packaging and presentation thereof can't make up if lacking in substance. Empathy, confidence.
Middle Managers	26 -34 35-44	Knowing the line between smart, sharp tailoring and flashy behavior. Composure, humour, empathy and a strong understanding of the present and what is needed to achieve a successful future strategy. Listening, decisive, gravitas, confidence, collaborative, passion, unafraid, realistic, visionary. Relationship builder.

		Credibility and proven.
		Respect shown for those they lead.
	45-54	Clear thinker and communicator/calm and considered.
		Passion, flair, imagination, honesty, sensitivity, charm, kindness. Honesty, integrity, sensitivity – being 'human'.
	65+	I believe in what you are saying. I believe that it can be achieved. I trust you. I will listen when you start to speak.
		Reliable, trustworthy, knowledgeable, considerate, good communicator, articulate. Politically astute.

Specialist	35-44	Centered, considered, listener, eye contact, confident, calm, pleasant, intelligent, good listener, pragmatic, approachable, strong-willed and determined. Being genuine. Art of listening. Empathy with employees.
	45-54	Confident, showing humility and a sense of humour. Being accessible. Calm confidence. Charisma. Considered, strong, believable, sympathetic, authoritative, fluid, and commanding. Personal enjoyment of job or appearance of it. Sense of humour. Empathy for the company, as in the people that you are with.
Team Member	35-44	Gravitas, vision, integrity, connects with their people, makes strong decisions, communicates clearly and often, knows the landscape,

		inspiring, considered, measured. Charisma.
	45-54	A commanding presence. Intelligent. Good at communicating with people. Has energy and drive. Honesty.

As the results of my survey revealed, there are a number of consistent words or phrases which were used to describe how those leaders who 'have it', and how others experience them. So let's begin this story by exploring the meaning of 'Executive Presence' and kick the tyres a bit more regarding what the results revealed. Below is *a selection* of some of the responses.

Confidence

The Oxford English Dictionary[3] includes within one of its definitions of 'confidence' the phrase 'the feeling or belief that one can have faith in or rely on someone or something'. I was curious to understand what confidence meant in the context of Executive Presence. Specifically, I discovered it was the ability of a leader to *command* attention but not to *demand* it. I love this distinction. Perhaps that's because of the connection that I make with Transactional Analysis and the notion of parent, adult and child behavior.

How many people can you think of whom – on closer scrutiny – demand attention all the time? They may be friends, family or clients but boy, there are a number of them around. I am forever discussing with my husband the number of people we know who have dreadful social skills and just bang on about themselves *all the time*. 'IAAM.com' stands for 'It's All About Me.com' and I have a colleague with whom I have collaborated and what I notice about him/her is the continual, unrelenting appetite to make him/her the centre of every conversation. It's exhausting; debilitating; boring to talk about just one person. And guess what? No one's that interesting. Really. Absolutely no-one.

A leader who commands confidence doesn't feel the need to be the centre of discussion or debate all the time. They're not necessarily the first to speak but when they do, others *want* to listen. Their tone, language, pace, content, approach, air of authority and crystal clear confidence means that others believe what they have to say.

Confidence within the context of Executive Presence also means that understated, calm, assured, controlled way of knowing – with certainty – what your talents, capabilities are – as well knowing what your gaps are. It's not about arrogance (i.e. I live with the burden of being perfect), it's more that level of honest, pragmatic, non-defensive and dare I say it – maturity - that comes with knowing that learning is a life-long journey. The intent isn't to be 'perfect', it's about being comfortable with knowing your strengths, and being open, willing and able to decide which flaws you want work on. In addition, when you make this part of your 'story' in a sincere, open fashion, it becomes even more engaging, persuasive, powerful and compelling.

Charisma

Charisma was once described to me as 'hard to define but you know it when you see it'. I love that. Our friends at the Oxford English Dictionary[114] would have us describe it as 'a compelling attractiveness or charm that can inspire devotion in others'. The research supported the view that charisma in leaders is essentially represented by people in two ways. Firstly, they are exceptionally skilled communicators and secondly, that they are able to connect with others at a deeper, more emotional level. Charismatic leaders from history, well, I wonder who you would turn to? Martin Luther King? John F. Kennedy? And others I am sure. The point is simply the way that charismatic leaders communicate means that they can quickly build trust and loyalty in others. Having said all of this, it's important to stress the need for individuality in the context of charisma. There isn't just one way to do this. There's numerous ways to do so and it links profoundly with the need to be authentic.

Poise

Whenever I think of the word 'poise', I'm drawn to words like 'calm', 'confident', 'controlled', 'elegant', 'balanced' and 'graceful'. A lovely phrase I read and liked to describe 'poise' was a leader who has 'an easy self-assurance'. What a lovely phrase! Even so, if we're talking about poise, it's not necessarily a word that is automatically associated with leadership, but my view is that this is critical for leaders who have 'presence'. Why? Well here's the thing. I think it's (relatively) easier to be able to be persuasive, engaging and all the way round impressive when you've had eight hours sleep, know your topic inside out, are rehearsed, facing a benign audience and are on the top of your game. It's much harder to 'do poise' when you've barely slept, haven't seen the pitch deck before facing a hostile audience who are baying for blood and quite frankly, have absolutely no idea what you're talking about. To cap it all off, if you throw into the mix the fact that you've had the time allocated to present to your audience reduced (which may not be a bad thing under the circumstances), but even so, it's all a nightmare. The phrase 'grace under pressure' seems entirely appropriate under these circumstances.

One of the past experiences in my life was the opportunity to study Neuro Linguistic Programming (NLP) and explore how certain situations caused me to 'lack poise'. In a nutshell, it strikes me that being able to feel, own and convey poise depends on a number of different things, including how you feel about yourself and what you believe about yourself, as well as being able to access a place where you are able to respond positively versus react negatively. I have a great friend who also shared with me that she believes poise is a muscle that is developed through how we 'carry ourselves' during the 'pinch points' in life. Again, somehow that's pure gold to me.

I read an excellent blog post by Paula Gregorowicz[159] which sums up this topic and to whom I must credit the following paragraphs. Poise for leaders starts from the inside out. It is extremely difficult to have ease and grace if you spend your entire life raging a battle of wills internally. If you carry an array of limiting beliefs, spend an inordinate amount of negative self-talk, and generally the majority of time is spent not treating yourself well, it's hard to feel positive about yourself. In fact, it's exhausting. You try so hard to keep the parts of yourself you don't like at bay that you will undoubtedly engage in self-sabotaging behaviour. If you don't have all the poise you desire, shifting your relationship with yourself is the first place to start. Responsibility is literally the ability to respond. That means responding (empowering) versus reacting (dis-empowering) to life's events and the people around you. Have you ever had an emotion fueled knee-jerk reaction and then totally regretted it? (Haven't we all?) That is the trap of reacting in a nutshell. Someone says something or something happens and you get a surge of initial emotion and then unconsciously react by doing or saying something in return. Responding is the conscious version of reacting. You create space between the event and your response (even if it is just seconds) so that you can be at choice and do or say what serves the higher good of all involved.

Unless you are able to be still and grounded on a regular basis you will find it very difficult to create that space between event and response. In addition, if you have no experience with tapping into the power of stillness in ordinary situations it will be near impossible for you to tap into it at critical moments. You can't tap into what you don't know. You can't tap into a reserve that doesn't exist. So, when it comes time for peak performance or for handling a high stress situation, your mind will start running around like a chicken with its head cut off because you don't have any other tools at hand with which to deal with the situation.

Doesn't this just make absolute sense?

It is how you are on the inside that becomes real by how you show up on the outside. We've all seen people who carry themselves with such grace and confidence that it is like watching art in motion, right? That external appearance when married with a strong internal experience is what constitutes true poise. When you have that you are truly at choice and able to succeed on your own terms.

Humility

According to a wide variety of dictionary reference material, accepted wisdom would suggest that the word humility means 'having a modest or low view of one's own importance'. Being humble is part of having Executive Presence and yet I suppose that for some – this might not sit very well within the context of leadership because of fear of an inherent contradiction. By that I mean that there may be those of the view that humility is associated with weakness. If you are humble then you are someone who is unsure of themselves and actually someone who *lacks confidence*. In fact, you could argue that such a person could be easily taken for a ride because they lacked the skills to stand up for themselves. This is absolutely not what I found behind the mean of humility in this confidence. Actually, it would appear that humility is about being *confident enough* as a leader to recognize personal weaknesses. It's about a lack of self -delusion and the courage and faith to seek the help and support needed to grow as a person.

Not convinced? Okay, let's go to empirical data.

The Harvard Business Review[158] recently reported research completed by Catalyst, showing that humility is one of four critical leadership factors for creating an environment where employees from different demographic backgrounds feel included. It's a very interesting survey of more than 1,500 workers from

Australia, China, Germany, India, Mexico, and the United States. Effectively what was found was that when employees observed altruistic or selfless behavior in their managers — a style characterized by 1) acts of humility, such as learning from criticism and admitting mistakes); 2) empowering followers to learn and develop; 3) acts of courage, such as taking personal risks for the greater good; and 4) holding employees responsible for results — they were more likely to report feeling included in their work teams. This was true for both women and men. I love this and it reflects very closely what I have found from my research – but also based on my experience in working with clients.

And finally, if none of that works for you, let's just go for the sound bite. There's a great quote by Ken Blanchard that I love from his book, *The One Minute Manager*[150] that somehow seems perfect for this debate about humility. Blanchard states "People with humility do not think less of themselves; they just think about themselves less".

Credibility

As I have done so far with each of these components, let's start with some clarity on definitions. Being credible is about our ability to be convincing as a leader, being plausible, compelling and persuasive. Leaders who have credibility are believed, and trusted, both in the specifics of what they say and do, as well as being trusted in general as a person. Why does this matter? Perhaps it is because leaders who are successful *in the long term* have to have an ability to behave in ways that causes people to see them as credible. Indeed, the most profound and extensive evidence to support this necessity is for us to merely look back at what has happened at a global level over the course of the last seven to eight years. The worldwide financial crash stands as a lengthy and irrefutable testament to how financial leaders have categorically failed in this area. I realise that politics is a whole other area – but there's another example of massive failing in the arena of credibility. Whatever your preference in the world of politics, certainly in the western world, the voting public has never been more jaded, tired and cynical – with good reason. Political leaders are failing to be persuasive, plausible and convincing over time.

I was minded to explore what someone who conveys credibility as a leader actually does. The obvious and immediate points of reference are that they are consistent in both what they say and what they do. In addition, there's a notion of certainty. What I mean by that is that leaders who convey credibility are constant. In other words, there is not a continual changing of direction, opinion, perspective and approach. In a good way, credible leaders are consistent in their leadership style. Predictable yes perhaps, boring no.

It's also worth exploring the notion of honesty in the context of credibility. Leaders who are credible are honest to the degree that it's reasonably possible to be so. That may sound a bit peculiar, but there are so many occasions that I have worked with clients where it is patently obvious that it's *not appropriate* to share everything with their team. The reality is that leaders are often in a position whereby they cannot reveal everything they know to followers. In this sense honesty does not necessarily mean sharing everything (since some things often need to remain confidential). It does mean that what a manager can share is the truth, even if it may not be the whole truth.

In addition credibility and trustworthiness occur through personal contact, and effective interpersonal communication. For example, as we've indicated elsewhere, a responsive leader will be perceived as more credible and trustworthy as compared to a relatively non-responsive leader. And, a leader who knows when to interact face-to-face (rather than, let's say, via email) will tend to be seen as more credible, and inspire greater loyalty compared to a leader who uses (or misuses) technology-based communication.

Of course, there's much more to the psychology of creating credibility, but it can be boiled down to this: Employees and followers will watch the leader, and look for the degree to which the leader behaves in ways consistent with his or her expressed values. In other words, walking the talk, while a bit of a cliché, is absolutely critical.

Authentic

When I conducted my research into what the phrase 'Executive Presence' actually means, one of the words that came out time and again from the data was the word 'authentic'. I'd not particularly anticipated that this word would be so important – but there it was – stated repeatedly – bright and bold in my notes and refusing to go away. Being real; being true to yourself; being who you really are – not a 'fake' you – all of these sorts of verbatim were stated again and again from the people who were interviewed. Of course on reflection, this makes absolute sense – not least of which because, frankly, the image industry suffered a major dent to its credibility in the 80s and 90s from trying to make everyone be 'the same'. Look, I'm not talking about the big hair or unfeasible shoulder pads. Nor am I talking about the pastel suits for men combined with a tee shirt and shoes with no socks (it was Miami Vice[160] and the 1980's!!!!). It was of its time. As image and the importance of communication in leadership and in business became more prominent, there was a movement to state 'the one true way' to look, sound or act professionally. There were rules; there were 'dos and don'ts', there was a 'right' way and a 'wrong' way. However, like absolutely everything, if we don't recognize how the world has changed, then we become irrelevant, out-of-date, and obsolete. Of course there are undoubtedly some principles, in terms of personal impact, that it absolutely makes sense to honour, that's just sensible. However, I have never been more convinced that a 'one size fits all', 'cookie-cutter' approach to image and impact is just wrong. We are all different, unique, and extraordinary. We bring to our professional lives an exclusive history, a personality woven from a set of circumstances that cannot be replicated, a variety of skills, qualities and flaws all of which make us exactly who we are. And exactly like absolutely no other person on the planet. If we ignore that, if we don't understand that, if we assume that everyone is the same, then we entirely miss the point. The world in which we live now requires a more nuanced, thoughtful, flexible approach.

And as I reflect on the word 'authentic' still further, I am reminded of how regularly I am asked the question which connects with the word 'authentic'. Often when talking with professionals about the concept of 'Personal Brand' I am regularly asked: "can you have one brand at work and another at home?" And my answer is always 'well, yes I suppose you could; but the question is – why would you want to?" Why would any leader want to bring 'one version of themselves' to work, and yet take an entirely different version of themselves home with them for life outside of work? Why? Isn't that odd? Isn't that just double the effort? Plus, what about your team? Don't you just want to credit them with a tiny bit more intelligence than that? Don't you think that they can't see through 'fake'? In my experience – they can and they do. And then we wonder why we can't seem to get the levels of engagement, commitment and loyalty that we need in order to grow the business.

It turns out that there is a whole philosophy and school of thinking which lends itself to the phrase 'authentic leadership'. A wide variety of worthy tomes encourage us to bring our best, true, real selves to work. We want to do that, don't we? Or else isn't it all just all one big game? So I got to thinking about the word 'authentic' and what that really means – and I explored still further what my research revealed and a number of points became clear. Authentic leaders are:

- **Congruent.** Authentic leaders know who they really are – the good, the bad and the ugly. They have a sincere, realistic and clear sense of their own good points as well as their flaws. They know they're not the finished article; and they know that they've still got work to do; but they're okay with that; and they're going to keep working on it. They're aware of their strengths and they continually want to work on their gaps/weaknesses or flaws. When you think about that – isn't that philosophy so inspiring? 'I'm not perfect; but I'm good at some things; and others I'm working on, or letting go of because I will find talent who are much better than I could ever be.' Who *wouldn't* want to work for a boss who thinks like that? I once worked for a leader who suffered from what I called the 'Jesus Christ' syndrome. He genuinely thought that no matter what role, function or activity there was within his business, he was the man to do it. He was the best at everything. How absolutely extraordinary is that? He was perfect; everyone else in his organization wasn't and he had to live with the reality and unending frustration from his perspective of just simply being that much better than everyone else. Of course this wasn't really true. He was a legend in his own lunchtime. What he really needed to be (and wasn't) was inspirational. A leader not an 'over contributor'. A coach not a 'do-er'. A supporter not a pedant. He needed to *lead*. Nothing wrong with challenging and stretching people (he did a lot of that), but without being a motivational, appreciative coach as well then engagement evaporates and people leave. Which they did (and continue to do). Talk about delusional.

- **Results focused** – naturally authentic leaders want to deliver; they've got to be able to deliver the numbers.

- **The heart counts** – in other words, it's not just about the head. Being able to connect with emotion and have emotional intelligence is *essential*. Authentic leaders have empathy, compassion, kindness, self-awareness, humility, forgiveness, self-deprecation, loyalty, passion, belief and conviction. They have vulnerability. They know they're not perfect – and sometimes they let the side down. But they've built up enough credit in the bank for their colleagues, team and organization to forgive them. They have emotional intelligence and a radar that's 'on'. They get that people are deeply flawed; and that we're all looking to 'belong' to something. They understand that if you want to get the best from people you need to connect to their emotion, not just their logic.

- **Vulnerable** – back to this word once again. It's so important that I'm going to talk about this in more detail. Vulnerability is about being willing to show their foibles. Willing not to be perfect and willing to show those around them that they aren't. The brilliant Brené Brown's book 'Daring Greatly'[35] talks at length about this. We aren't perfect. None of us. Get over it if you hadn't realized before just now and think about how you can use your vulnerability to bring deeper and more meaningful connection to those around you. That's compelling; that's engaging and that's persuasive. And that's Executive Presence.

Self-Awareness

I have had a number of conversations recently with super smart, high potential talent. These are people with a boatload of qualifications, brains the size of small plants and more analytical skills than you can shake a stick at. I distinctly recall a conversation with an MBA graduate who was assigned to me for an Executive Coaching engagement. This had been combined with a 360-assessment process and the critical messages were simply: bright, smart, clever, brilliant analytical skills - and low emotional intelligence. For this candidate, working harder wasn't necessary, being smarter wasn't necessary... but what *was* necessary was the need for him to develop a set of softer skills that he simply had not paid sufficient attention to during his career to date. It was an extremely hard concept for him to grasp (and I always find that utterly astonishing for such an intellectually bright individual). What he hadn't, as yet, grasped is the simple fact that leadership is a relationship business. Being bright, smart, clever and highly analytical will get you so far. And then it won't do a thing for you. I'll say it again: leadership is a relationship business. The best, most brilliant leaders with exquisite influencing skills understand this simple premise. There comes a point where leaders deliver through the results, efforts and commitment of others. That means a set of 'people skills' that are simply outstanding.

In 2013, Forbes.com quoted a fascinating study that explored the notion of leadership and self-awareness. The study was conducted in 2010 by Green Peak Partners[111] and Cornell's School of Industrial and Labor Relations[104] and it was cited by the American Management Association on Twitter. The study examined 72 executives at public and private companies with revenues from $50 million to $5 billion. The research examined a number of executive interpersonal traits, and here's a quote that aligns very much with my research around Executive Presence. Namely:

"Leadership searches give short shrift to 'self-awareness,' which should actually be a top criterion.

Interestingly, a high self-awareness score was the strongest predictor of overall success. This is not altogether surprising as executives who are aware of their weaknesses are often better able to hire subordinates who perform well in categories in which the leader lacks acumen. These leaders are also more able to entertain the idea that someone on their team may have an idea that is even better than their own."

I have been involved in a global initiative in the car-manufacturing sector and the purpose of it is to explore the level of employee engagement that exists within dealerships across the country. Why care? Because what is proven, beyond all doubt, is that employees who are more engaged at work, deliver more effective levels of service to customers. They, in turn, are more engaged in the dealership and display higher levels of loyalty, as well as advocating on behalf of the dealership. The point is this; time again, what is absolutely apparent is that when surveying employees, those leaders who had high levels of self-awareness genuinely had more impact and made more progress to drive commercial imperatives within the dealership.

Daniel Goleman, in his superb book 'Emotional Intelligence'[112], reinforces the absolute necessity to be able to 'read others', and gauge self. The way that he terms it is the ability to develop 'social awareness' by being able to read the room, and then be able to gauge the effect of yourself on others, which Goleman terms 'self awareness'. There's something quite damning about saying 'you need to develop social skills', but in essence, that's what my client needs to do if he wants to become an exceptional manager.

The more I talk and write about self-awareness, the more passionate and enthusiastic I become about it. The thing is, everything starts with how well we know ourselves. How connected we are to what really represents our strengths, and how honest we are about what really does de-rail us. In a Harvard Business Review article, *"Managing Oneself,"*[113] Peter Drucker wrote, "Whenever you make a decision or take a key decision, write down what you expect will happen. Nine or 12 months later, compare the results with what you expected." Drucker called this self-reflection process *feedback analysis* and credited it to a 14th-century German theologian. He said it was the "only way to discover your strengths." Many successful leaders follow similar practices: Warren Buffett, for example, has made it a habit for years to write down the reasons why he is making an investment decision and later look back to see what went right or wrong. The point is, being self-aware, being socially aware, knowing our impact and effect on others – be it in an everyday conversation – or be it at a more intrinsic level – the point is those leaders with Executive Presence have a very sensitive level of awareness, and are willing (and able) to make the necessary adjustments.

Life-Long Learning

There are amongst leaders with Executive Presence not only an awareness of strengths and flaws, but also a passion, interest and appetite to want to continually learn and develop over the course of their career. It's not the case of somehow reaching a level that means that learning is no longer necessary. Mark Miller co-authored a great book with Ken Blanchard called *The Secret: What Great Leaders Know and Do*[115]. It reinforces the notion that the most successful leaders are committed to a continual path of learning over the course of their career.

Integrity

Just to mix things up a bit I have referenced a different dictionary source for this word. According to dictionary.com[116] integrity is 'adherence to moral and ethical principles; soundness of moral character; honesty'. Perhaps we should not be surprised at the prevalence of this characteristic within our definition. As leaders, our challenge is to do the right thing, every time, no matter the consequences. For me it's a bit like culture. It's what we do when we think no one is looking. In the book *The Leadership Challenge*[117] James Kouzes and Barry Posner have researched integrity in leadership and its significance for success. The characteristic found to be most important was honesty. Our belief in leaders within society has never been more sorely tested and I have provided an (almost depressing) list of recent examples of scandals across society in Chapter 5.

What This All Means

So these words are the key, consistent and continual phrases that were revealed when our survey respondents were asked, 'What is Executive Presence?' I could go on and on. Just reflect on what's been written. That's a big ask as leaders, isn't it? And it's not easy in terms of being able to communicate it consistently, continually and congruently. It prompted me to want to understand how to achieve this and create a framework for doing so. I have created a model – based on the research – that identifies the critical elements of Executive Presence at which we, as leaders, need to excel. Why? Because if we do, we can engage, ignite and motivate those around us to achieve results in times of change and uncertainty. And, when I wrote that, the title of the book was finalized.

The Model For Executive Presence - LEADER

Look	How you appear; your visual signature; dressing to your essence; putting consistent intention and alignment into your look.

Engage	How you connect with emotion; winning hearts and minds; how you attract, inspire, challenge, support, motivate, develop and influence others.
Act	How you behave; your non-verbal communication; how you strategize with your physical presence; using your body to support, not subtract, from your verbal message.
Deliberate	How you think; your preferences for processing information; how you make decisions, solve problems, manage complexity, prioritize, strategize and rationalize business issues.
Evolve	How you maximize your potential, how you manage your career, your locus of control, finding and pursuing your passion, succeeding at your life's purpose.
Resonate	How you sound; how you maximize the qualities of your voice to suit the occasion and audience; how you convey clarity, relevance, precision and brilliance through your verbal messages.

Each of the following chapters explores the model in more detail and critically, provides a range of skills and strategies, tools and techniques to communicate it. Remember, you can dip into the chapter that appeals most to you or you can be very old school about it and start at 'Look' and read forward from there. In any event, you are invited to sit back, relax and enjoy the discussion.

Chapter Four –
The Look of a Leader

*"Because the first thing we see when you walk in the door **isn't** your talent, wit, personality, intellect, wisdom or domain expertise"*

Sarah Brummitt

Why You Need to Care about Your 'Look'

How you look matters as a leader, as an influencer and as a successful professional - whether you like it or not. It's part of your influencing toolkit and we need to end all of the noise and distraction that tries to suggest to the contrary. There are a myriad of different reasons why, as a leader, you need to care about how you convey your 'visual signature' and this is not about vanity, indulgence, narcissism or celebrity. Don't just take my word for it. The research shows that how you look is an important component to the 'executive presence' you convey.

What We Asked and What the Research Revealed

Reminding you of one of the questions posed from the survey was this:

How important is a Leader's image and appearance to your perception of them professionally?

Respondents answered across the following scale:

- *Extremely important*
- *Important*
- *Moderately important*
- *Slightly important*
- *Not important at all*

83% of respondents said that a leader's image and appearance was either extremely important or important to the professional perception of them. Only 2% said that it was not important at all. So, let's be clear: what you wear and how you look matters when it comes to your ability to convey Executive Presence.

When respondents were asked the following:

Put these factors into the order of their importance for being an effective leader, where 1 is the most important and 5 is the least important:

- *How a leader looks*
- *How a leader connects with those they are leading*
- *How a leader behaves*
- *How a leader thinks and makes decisions*
- *How a leader verbally communicates*

My research asked the question 'what is most important to convey 'Executive Presence'? There were five categories from which to choose and the 'ability to connect emotionally with people' was deemed to be most important of the five categories. Interestingly, how a leader looks was rated the least important of these five categories. *However,* before we run away with the idea that image *isn't important,* 83% of respondents said how leaders look was either extremely important or important to the professional perception of a leader. This reinforces that image is a vital component to our perception of others as a professional leader. (As an additional note, if 83% of respondents who thought how a leader looks was either extremely important or important to the professional perception of a leader and this was ranked fifth out of five, then just think how important the other categories are when it comes to impact on the perception of us as a professional leader.)

There were 7% of females who responded and they place how a leader looks as *the most important factor* to conveying Executive Presence. 0% of men placed the look of a leader as the most important factor. Overall, 85% of the women who responded thought the look of a leader was extremely important or important as opposed to 80% men. In terms of anything interesting to report when it comes to perceptions between the genders, there was a very slight tendency for women to place greater significance on this factor than men.

We also explored specific factors within the area of Image/Appearance to see if specifics about appearance could be discerned. Specifically:

- *Quality clothing*
- *Sharp tailoring*
- *Wearing a tie (gentlemen)*
- *Wearing a jacket*
- *Wearing a skirt or dress (ladies)*
- *Wearing bold colours/style*
- *Showing attention to detail in appearance*
- *Wearing current fashion*
- *Expensive clothing accessories (i.e. shoes, watch, jewellery)*
- *High quality business accessories (i.e. briefcase or bag, laptop, mobile, phone, pen)*
- *Immaculate grooming*

Three key areas were revealed as statistically *most important.* These were quality clothing, attention to detail and immaculate grooming. In detail, 72.8% of respondents thought that quality clothing was either extremely important or important. Perhaps not surprisingly, wearing current fashions were deemed to be least important. Attention to detail and immaculate grooming were actually joint second. The remainder of responses, in order was:

4. Sharp tailoring
5. Wearing a jacket
6. High quality business accessories (iPad, phone etc.)
7. Wearing a tie
8. Wearing a skirt
9. Wearing bold colours
10. Expensive clothing accessories (handbag, wallet)
11. Wearing current fashion

It's Instinctive

But in addition to my research, what other reasons can we point to in order to underscore the importance of image? Here's the reality. We have all evolved from the animal kingdom and our natural, instinctive reaction *every time we see each other* is to check each out and make sure we are not a 'threat'. This is just about survival. This really does apply to you! I'll survey you from top to toe when we meet and absorb what I see. I do it all the time; every day and every single-sighted person on the planet will do it. I will take onboard this visual information and use it as a first point of calibration for what you represent in that moment. Remember – so do you.

This leads nicely to my next point, which is Malcolm Gladwell's stunning book *Blink*[110], in which he noted the phrase 'thin slicing'. Effectively 'thin slicing' is frameworks for explaining what many different empirical studies have already proved. That the way humans operate is to take very small windows of observation, (in other words very small amounts of information – or thin slices), and use this to make decisions and reach conclusions. These brief, near instantaneous decisions tend to remain unchanged, the longer we are exposed to whatever it is. In other words, what we think based on small pieces of information can have a very dramatic impact on the impression we create. Within three seconds I need to decide if you have the capability to be credible. Within 30 seconds I need to decide if your point of view is one that I want to consider and within three minutes I have a number of very firm opinions on you, your story and whatever recommendations you may be making. I'll decide if I want to be persuaded to your point of view or not.

Competence Is A Given

Moving on, can we just get over the whole 'style over substance' argument? Let's be clear. I'm *assuming* that you are technically superb at your job. In other words, whether you are a marketer, an engineer, a procurement specialist, an accountant, a sales professional, a lawyer or whatever your chosen profession, I'm assuming that you're already *really, really good at it*. If you're not, then you don't need this book; what you need to do instead is build the domain strength you need in your chosen profession first. Without that, your ability to influence and have presence is simply non-existent. As a professional, if you have the reputation of being perceived as poor at your job, then you can forget being influential unless, and until, you've fixed this by firstly, developing your technical skills.

Another angle on this whole 'how I look doesn't matter' delusion is this. Please remember that you cannot afford to fall into the trap of thinking that if you *are* really skilled technically in your chosen profession, then you have influence. It doesn't matter that you don't care about how you look; you're brilliant and the rest of us will just have to live with it. This outlook on life and business is at best naïve and at worst simply dangerous and self-destructive. Being technically brilliant is your ticket to the game; it doesn't mean you'll win the match. Leadership is a relationship business and relationships are built on the ability to be influential. Your image is part of how you influence others and if you really want to be influential, you need to hone exquisite influencing skills – and image is part of that skill set.

We All Have Expectations

No matter where we live in the world, we all have certain expectations around how people of authority, influence and power should dress. Yes, there is a wide range of industry, cultural, seasonal and practical considerations to throw into the mix – but no matter where you live and what industry in which you work, what you wear says a lot about you. Those individuals who are perceived to have influence, authority and 'power' are also expected to dress in a certain way to reinforce these messages.

On that point, and before you jump up and down and start pointing to successful entrepreneurs who have been phenomenally effective (Richard Branson, Steve Jobs etc.) and yet who seem to break all the 'rules' in terms of dress code, let me continue. *All* leaders set a tone and culture in which they make it *extremely clear* the role that clothing plays within their business. In other words, they *prove* my point; not disprove it. Apple is a casual work environment and if, as a man, you walked into their offices wearing a chalk stripe navy suit with white shirt and tie, you would look totally out of place. In other words, if you went there dressed as if you were going to a financial institution in the City, then you would convey no credibility, authority or influence with that get up, that's for sure. Equally, if you wore a black pullover, jeans and trainers - for which Steve Jobs was renowned, and indeed that was *his* visual signature - to work in a London law firm, you'd achieve *exactly the same result.* In other words, the lawyers in that law firm would perceive you to have no authority, no influence or power because of your sartorial choice either. Quite simply their expectations and cultural norms as a business will have been greatly disappointed.

As an aside, what I do concede is that when you're as successful as the likes of Richard Branson et al, you can wear what the hell you like. It's your business and you can do whatever you want. However for the rest of us - and there are quite a lot people who would fall into the category of 'the rest of us' - the reality is that we can't adhere to the same rules. Sorry, but we can't. We need to understand that in the absence of the meteoric success of Messrs.' Branson, Jobs et al, we have to understand the part our 'look' or visual signature plays in our ability to influence and we need to leverage it to our advantage.

Science Supports the Psychology of Dressing

There are a number of different studies that support the notion of clothing being able to impact our thinking and the way in which our brain works. In July 2012, Hajo Adam and Adam D. Galinsky published a paper in the Journal of Experimental Social Psychology[71]. Essentially they were looking to test the psychological impact of wearing different types of clothing. Their view is that wearing certain clothes has two impacts – which are both separate and connected. The first is the symbolism in the clothing, in other words what it means to the wider world when we wear particular garments. The second is then the physical impact of wearing such items. Three different experiments around wearing a white coat (symbolizing carefulness and attentiveness) were conducted and what they revealed was fascinating. Wearing a laboratory coat increases attention, however, wearing the same white coat did not increase when it was associated with a painter. It only increased when wearing the coat was associated with a doctor. Their conclusion was that the influence of clothing depends on both *wearing them* and also the symbolism of them when you are wearing them.

And it would appear that they are not alone.

Psychologist Abraham Rutchick from California State University published research in 2015[72]. His research suggests that wearing a suit, for example, can change the way you are perceived by others and in addition, broaden your thinking. The premise of the original study was to test participants' thought patterns in relation to the formality of their clothing. One of the findings was that those individuals who wore a suit *felt* more powerful and this encouraged them to conduct more 'abstract processing' behaviour. 'Abstract processing' to you and I is where we think more strategically rather than at a detailed, tactical level. This research is fascinating, not least because it tests the theory in an ever more casual work environment that it doesn't matter what we wear.

Organizations now are encouraging more home working so clothing might be even less relevant. Not so says Rutchick. "Putting on more formal clothes makes us feel more powerful, and that changes the basic way we see the world." [72] Rutchick conducted two experiments, the first of which required students to wear whatever they chose, rather the formality of it and then complete a number of cognitive tests designed to measure how they processed information (i.e. whether it was in an abstract or concrete way). The researchers initially found that those individuals who rated their outfits as more formal, were more likely to think in an abstract way as compared to those individuals who rated their outfits as casual wear. Given that the initial research was completed on campus, not many individuals typically wore a suit, and so for the next three experiments, half of the students were then asked to change into suits before being subjected to more tests. Again, those individuals in suits demonstrated more abstract thinking and also felt more powerful.

Why does wearing a suit make a difference to how we think? Although there is a lack of evidential proof, what social psychologists will say is that if we know we look good, we feel a stronger sense of being in control, or at the top of our game. What this might engender is a strong sense of confidence and power –

and it is that which is linked to thinking in an abstract
way.

Get It Right and We Notice You; Get It Wrong and We Notice the Clothes

Why else does your 'look' as a leader matter? Quite
simply, when you get it right, we notice the person
and when you get it wrong, we notice the clothes.
Time and time again there have been endless
examples of what happens when leaders get it wrong
and my point is, that's what gets noticed and gets
written about in the media. Not the person or the issue
or the priority but the clothes. In 1981, Michael Foot,
the then leader of the Opposition Labour Party in the
UK wore an industrial garment (otherwise known as a
'donkey' jacket') to a Service of Remembrance at the
Cenotaph in Whitehall, London. This service is a
national event held every November, where the nation
pauses to mark those who have fallen in service of
their country from two world wars, plus more recent
conflicts in the Middle East. It's a somber, respectful,
reflective occasion where the nation pays their
respects to the war dead. Michael Foot, as one of the
politicians of the time who was involved in the
service, looked as if he didn't care. His choice of
garment sent a very clear message to the media and
the nation – whether he meant that or not. My
supposition is that he did not intend to cause the furore
and offence that he did. However, the nation looked
on aghast and inferred significant meaning from his
choice of clothing, and none of it was positive.

An American Example

Here's another, more recent case in point. On Thursday, August 28th 2014, President Barack Obama conducted a press conference at the White House. Nothing unusual about that, of course, but it had been a very grim week for the USA with an American being beheaded, the advance of ISIS had continued and a further crisis escalation was unfolding in Ukraine. The news was grim frankly, a relentless and depressing tide of news which would test the reserves of the most optimistic souls. Now I said that there was nothing unusual about Obama addressing the press corps – which was true – except for one thing that was extraordinarily different. The world's most powerful man was wearing a tan suit. Yes, you read that correctly. The world's most powerful man was wearing a tan suit. Social media exploded[10]. If you jump online and search for Republicans who had a view about this, it is almost funny to see the ire with which they responded to Obama's choice of attire[11]. The most powerful man in the world looked like he was going to an Easter wedding, rather than heading into the White House briefing room to address the nation regarding hideously bleak news. Remember – when you get it right we notice you. When you get it wrong we notice the clothes.

Our Friends in Greece

As I write this book, yet another example has appeared in the media over the last few days. Yanis

Varoufakis is the Greek Finance Minister who had embarked upon a European tour in February and March 2015 with the sole purpose of engaging the rest of the European Union with the concept of extending the conditions of the Greek bailout to avoid Greece reneging on their repayment obligations and effectively going bankrupt. So, by anyone's standards the purpose of his trip is extremely serious. However, Varoufakis has appeared on the steps of 11 Downing Street to a photo opportunity with the UK Chancellor of the Exchequer George Osborne[144]. For this occasion he chose to wear a blue, open-neck shirt, casual trousers, no formal jacket and unfortunately an overcoat that bears more than a passing resemblance to the 'donkey jacket' garment, which seems to have reappeared once more. Why did he do that? What message did he want to convey? Do we really want to be distracted by what he's wearing because it simply doesn't align with our expectations of a European leader, who is representing a country in crisis and where *he needs to convey* that he's got the credibility to get a grip of the situation and resolve it? His attire distracted us all because it didn't match our expectations and that's exactly my point. Get it right and we notice the person (issue/priority). Get it wrong and we notice the clothes. If you think clothes shouldn't be the main topic of discussion (and I am also one of these people), then learn to get it right, rather than thinking it doesn't matter and therefore continuing to get it wrong.

We Also Get It Wrong in the UK

In March 2015, George Osborne, Chancellor of the Exchequer in the UK, stood up in the House of Commons to present the last pre-election budget. Osborne is a member of the Conservative Party, who has just spent five years in a coalition government with the Liberal Democrats. Social media went mad[1]; not because of the economic policies that he was announcing, but rather, as he stood at the dispatch box and addressed political friends and foes alike, with a live feed of his speech broadcasting on the mainstream 24 hour TV news channels in the UK, the whole topic of discussion was his suit. Yes, his suit. The very next day, one of the most supportive broadsheet newspapers of the Conservative Party, The Daily Telegraph[2], came out and wrote at length about his sartorial choice. Boy, did they have a lot of material to work with. An extremely short, super narrow lapel (described by one online wag as 'a suit from Baby Gap'), combined with the most absurdly short trousers that revealed far too much of his leg when he walked. Now, given that the UK has been in one of the most economically austere periods since the Second World War, with deep and extensive economic cuts across vast swathes of society, this sartorial 'faux pas' invites commentary and ridicule around the extent of the cuts now extending to the Chancellor of the Exchequer's trousers. Osborne's whole visual signature underscored a schoolboy impression visually and conveyed many (negative) messages: immature, thoughtless, poor attention to detail (not good when you're talking about numbers), inappropriate, and woefully lacking in credibility. It's a distraction; it's unhelpful and my point is that it is completely avoidable.

And I'm Not Just Picking on the Men

'Newsnight'[161] is a flagship, late-night television show that is broadcast by the BBC in the UK. One of its presenters is Emily Maitlis, a superb, intelligent, articulate, multi-lingual journalist and broadcaster. I admire her professionally and she has a reputation for being a thoughtful and incisive interviewer who can challenge the thinking of any politician whom she interviews. In March 2015, the election 'silly season' started. Endless debates, interviews and manifesto rhetoric from all political parties as they attempted to secure our vote. So that's the context. On one show, Maitlis chose to wear a shirt with a tie that was undone, a waistcoat, skinny jeans and open toes boots. Now, as a dramatic wardrobe dresser, I liked the outfit as a concept. However was it appropriate? Social media went mad[9]. Endless comparisons were drawn between her choice of outfit and the typical St. Tinian's, schoolgirl get up. And those comparisons would be fair. It just wasn't appropriate for the occasion, environment, her goals (I am certain she does not want to be perceived to dress like a rebellious schoolgirl) and so on.

Remember, None of This is about Fashion

Look, I could go on and on about examples from the world of politics. Seriously, there is a vast and unending wealth of material from which to draw. The beauty of politics is that there is a forum to reflect what individual voters may well be thinking – and that is the media. When talking about a leader's visual signature I deliberately don't reference the world of celebrity because this *is not* about style. This *is not* about fashion. This *is not* frivolous, vacuous or pointless. The visual signature of our political leaders should be such that it aligns with, rather than contradicts, the messages about their talent, policies and ability to run our state, republic or country. They are trying to influence us; let's be clear. The same philosophy is absolutely true for leaders in business. So, as a professional, your visual signature needs to align with (rather than contradict) the messages about your talent, your approach and your ability to run a team, department or organization.

We Don't all Have To Dress the Same

As my lengthy answer continues as to the reasons why we need, as professionals and leaders, to consider how we appear, let me address another query that is regularly posed in relation to this specific topic. Considering how you dress and appear *is not* about trying to encourage all professionals to wear the same thing. This *is not* about trying to drive uniformity (literally and metaphorically). The working environment in which we operate has never been more disparate and casual, so that won't work for a start. However, in addition, let's talk about you as a person. Everyone is different. We bring to work a unique career history, experience, level of skills, personality, attitude and level of engagement for what we do on a daily basis. Being influential is about understanding how to *leverage that positively* through your appearance. It's about being you, even when faced with 'guidelines' at work regarding what is and what is not deemed to be acceptable. I believe strongly in the concept of individuality, and there are so many options to convey that visually. When working with professional men and women, one of my first questions is to understand what individuals want to convey in terms of their personal brand (because they've got one – like it or not). I want to know what my clients want the world to think when they walk in the room. And then I'm keen to look to support that through the choices they make with their visual appearance.

All Facets of our Communication Have to 'Add Up'

And finally - although I am tempted to wonder if you *really do* need more reasons why - if the visual, verbal and non-verbal facets of communication are not aligned, then we don't trust the overall message being communicated. In other words, if I look good but the way I speak isn't convincing, or if the content of what I say doesn't make sense, then we don't trust the message. Or, if my verbal communication is good, I look fine but my non-verbal communication is nervous, lacking in confidence or negative, then we don't trust the message. Quite simply, if it doesn't all add up, then we just don't buy it. So, all the facets of my communication must make sense in order to be believed – and that includes my image or 'look' as a leader.

Even In Business We Are Influenced By What's Going on Outside It

In the 1980s we all looked ridiculous. I know, because I've seen the photos of me in more shoulder pads, boxy jackets, long length pleated skirts and cone heels than you could shake a stick at. All topped off with a ridiculous perm. Aaron Spelling's TV shows[162] were everywhere and the likes of 'Dallas', 'Knots Landing', 'Beverley Hills 90210', 'Falcon Crest', and 'Dynasty' reinforced a look that was glamorous, wealthy, dramatic and bold. The impact that these TV shows had on what we wore was extraordinary. I know I wasn't the only one who chose to dress as I did and whilst it's both easy and very amusing to look back and laugh, the reality is that a lot of drama, angles, bold colours, high accent accessories were being worn for a glamorous, alluring (but not very credible), professional look. By the way, for the men amongst you who might be sat there smugly thinking 'yes, those chicks got it wrong but I didn't', you are not going to get off quite so lightly. I've got two words to say to you about the cultural influences that undoubtedly impacted how you dressed: '*Miami Vice*'[160].

In any event, this decade – and in actual fact as we transitioned into the 1990s - was characterized by dressing for a 'power look'. I have already mentioned the ubiquitous shoulder pads (for men and women), a tailored work look of which served to underscore the capitalist, aspirational, entrepreneurial political landscape driven by Margaret Thatcher and Ronald Reagan of the time – both in the US and in Europe. At the time, this was perfectly fine, and yet (and perhaps as you can tell), professional men and women were crying out for some clarity on what to wear. Perhaps unsurprisingly, there was a real movement to start to provide guidance around how to 'dress for success'. John T. Molloy's eponymous book[163] was, in fact, an incredibly valuable contribution to the discussion regarding what to wear for work. Most people really didn't know what the 'rules' or considerations were around how to dress for a wide range of business situations.

My hope is that for all of these different reasons, you are now persuaded that the look of a leader is an important component to their presence. Sometimes the image industry has suffered some bad press over the years and as an image professional, I can say that our industry has some responsibility for this being so. In essence, whether we like it or not, and for all these different reasons, our 'look' matters. So, let's get to some definitions of 'look' when it comes to Executive Presence.

The 'L' in LEADER Stands for 'Look'

My research clearly reveals that how we look is an important component to our ability to influence others. The 'L' in my 'LEADER' model for Executive Presence stands for the 'Look' of a leader. Specifically this means:

'How you appear; your visual signature; dressing to your essence; putting consistent intention and alignment into your look'

Avoiding the 'Yes, But' Game

Before we get started, a note of caution. When I first started advising professional men and women on image, I became aware of a select group of individuals who played the 'yes, but' game. Here's what I mean by that: essentially, taking anything I said and then trying really hard to find a way to disprove it; through a convoluted set of circumstances. Yes, if your client is a travelling circus operating in Eastern Europe then this advice on how to dress might not apply in the same way, but let's just get real. What is set out over the next few pages is *a wide range of choice*, rather than a list of 'you must, must not' statements. This is about providing an extensive array of well-researched, empirically sound information from which to pick and choose in order to create the presence you want.

Getting the 'Look' Right Consistently

I would suggest that there are six core principles to consistently dressing well as a leader and if you unswervingly honour these, then you will always dress appropriately, authentically and effectively to convey presence, gravitas and impact – no matter the situation. These principles are:

- Evolve Your Visual Signature
- Decide What's Appropriate
- Know What's Complementary
- Wear The Right Colour
- Complete Immaculate Grooming
- Pay Attention To Details

Quite simply, as a leader, if we want to convey Executive Presence then we need to **look like a leader**. What do you want us to see when you walk in the room? We need, visually, to communicate a look that aligns with, rather than contradicts all of our professional capabilities and personal qualities, and hence what we choose to wear needs to honour these six principles. We will take each in turn.

Evolve Your Visual Signature

Dolly Parton once said that "it costs a lot of money to look this cheap"[126]. She undoubtedly has a signature style, which may or may not be to our taste. In the world of business there are many, many examples of leaders who have evolved their own visual signature. Steve Jobs[127] is an obvious one. He always wore a black turtleneck sweater, jeans and New Balance sneakers. At one level many have tried to argue that he didn't care about how he looked. I would argue the complete opposite. His look was very much in line with the Silicon Valley, west coast, Internet, hi-tech casual vibe, but also it conveys confidence and was highly memorable. It also aligned with simplicity of the design aesthetic for his products. Mark Zuckerberg[128] from Facebook is another example of this. He always wears a grey tee. Anna Wintour[129], the Artistic Director of Conde Nast Publications (think Vogue), is always in dark glasses. Even indoors when in the pitch black and watching a runway show, Michael Kors[164] always wears the same thing. Simon Cowell[130] always wears one of two different outfits (grey V-neck tees and jeans or white shirt with a black suit). Martin Bell[131] is a BBC correspondent and former Member of Parliament in the United Kingdom who always wears a white suit, which he deems as lucky. What's the point of all these examples? I'm not actually suggesting you wear exactly the same items all the time. I am suggesting you evolve a look or style that is authentic, relevant, distinct and obvious to the brand you want to communicate and the presence you want to convey. What do you want to communicate visually that makes you 'you'?

Decide What's 'Appropriate'

'Appropriate' is such a great word; not least because it's a word that everyone understands whilst simultaneously having very little idea of what it means when it comes to applying it to business attire. The New Oxford English Dictionary[3] explains that 'appropriate' means 'suitable or proper in the circumstances'. I'm not really sure that definition gets us any further. What do I think it means? I think that the word 'appropriate' in relation to your choice of attire at work is based on a number of specific criteria. Namely:

- **Your goals** for the interaction (i.e. what you want to achieve). Is it a decision? Greater trust? More conversation? More credibility? Do you want them to be more persuaded by your point of view? Or something else?

- **The audience's expectations** of what you should wear for that interaction. Is this a formal pitch? Interview? Team meeting? What is the occasion for which communication with other people is required?

- The **time of day** (literally, day versus evening).

- The **geography** in which you are operating. How business attire looks in Bermuda (think shorts, long socks worn with jacket and shirt) is very different to the Middle East, the Far East, Western Europe and so on.

- The **climate** (and I do literally mean whether it's 100°C in the shade or whether it's -15°C) because that certainly has an impact on clothing choice.

- The **culture of the business** in which you are seeking to influence. This is about *the client's expectations* (not yours), based on their cultural norms, standards and expectations.

- Any **personal, cultural or religious considerations** that need to be honoured and respected through your attire. We live in a cosmopolitan, multi-cultural, connected business world and it would be foolish to ignore specific considerations of this nature.

- **The key messages** that you want the audience to infer from you as a professional person. What do you want the world to 'get' about you? (Remembering of course that one of the ways we 'get' you is by what we see.)

In many ways, I think dressing 'appropriately' is the hardest criterion to get consistently right – and what has made this even more so in today's business world, is the pervasive influence of 'business casual'. How we dress for work has fundamentally changed over the last twenty years and the confusion and chaos that this has the potential to cause is everywhere. Just check out what some people are wearing to work tomorrow to see my point proven. Of course, there are certain industries still formally uniformed, and there are others that still have a fairly traditional, conservative set of guidelines around what is worn to work, (for example in the UK this might include the finance sector and lawyers and I am sure our international readers can offer other examples from their world), but the majority of the Western business world has moved to business casual.

A Short Detour - the Backstory to 'Business Casual'

How on earth did we get to this point? In 2012, I had the privilege of going to Hawaii to present at an international image conference. Whilst I was there, I immersed myself in a wide range of local material – one of which proved to be so incredibly valuable to this book. It was a tourism leaflet that outlined the part that Hawaii played in the evolution of 'business casual'. It was brilliant for many reasons, not least of which because it explained how the evolution of business casual began – and it was a lot earlier than I had originally been led to believe. When I first started studying image, I distinctly remember being told that business casual came out of Silicon Valley as a rebellion to the formal 'dress for success' movement of the 1980s. Well, apparently there's more to it than that.

In clothing terms, Hawaii is known for one thing: shirts. Hawaiian shirts (otherwise known as Aloha shirts) were an important manufacturing product for the island and in 1966, the clothing industry in that part of the world was focused on trying to sell more of them. As a result, someone came up with the idea of 'Aloha Friday'. Doesn't that phrase just sound lovely by the way? Anyway, I digress. The idea behind 'Aloha Friday' was to encourage businesses to let their employees wear Hawaiian shirts to work one day a week. The result was quite simply something that started life as a marketing initiative to flog more shirts, simply morphed into a movement that was far more significant. It became part of the cultural norm, a rhythm of life on the island. Like clothing through the ages, the Hawaiian shirt was making a statement and that statement was to chill out, relax and remember that work isn't everything in life.

And it doesn't end there. When you think of 'business casual' attire – I defy you *not* to think of the button-down shirt and khaki trousers. What is true is that when in the 1990s times were more challenging economically, the 'business casual' look had become a 'no cost' perk for 'Corporate America'. Khaki trousers are smart, relaxed cut casual trouser worn by civilians, even though this particular garment has its origins in the military. Our fabulous friends in North America have nailed this look and it's one that is worn all over Corporate America to this day. What I hadn't appreciated was the reason behind the evolution of this particular style of trouser – because there is one.

Remember, the Hawaiian shirt was now increasingly common at work but the challenge was – what to wear with it? The baby boomer generation was getting larger and they were becoming less and less enthusiastic about the idea of wearing jeans.

In addition, Levi had bought a brand called 'Dockers' who manufactured what was effectively a golfing trouser and the company decided that if they were going to revive their fortunes – then what better way to do it than to encourage men to wear these trousers to the office. Dockers conducted an extensive marketing campaign with the phrase 'going from the golf course to the cubicle' was a mantra that supported a marketing campaign whereby HR Managers in the USA were aggressively and extensively campaigned with a 'Guide to Business Casual Dressing'. It outlined a number of different 'business casual' looks to help HR Managers in the guidance that they wrote and shared with their employees. Hence, the evolution of this cut of trouser meant a great alternative. This was so simple, but so very clever.

A footnote to this story is that Dockers themselves wanted to push back against the perception that they themselves described about the brand. Namely, that Dockers is now the uniform of the man who works in a 'cubicle'. They represent the attire of what became termed 'the guy who doesn't care'. As a result, they launched a type of trouser called the 'Alpha Pant'. I'm sorry, but this is a perfect example of a cross-cultural clash and in the UK we all know that pants mean undergarments. I'm sorry; I just couldn't stop laughing at the whole concept. It's absolutely hysterical. Essentially this detour down memory lane regarding the evolution of 'business casual' only serves to remind us that clothes communicate something about us – whether we like it or not.

So What *Is* 'Business Casual' in the 21st Century?

There are so many problems with the phrase 'business casual', not least the fact that it is an oxymoron. When asking clients for definitions I am regularly faced with replies that speak of what *cannot* be worn rather than garments and accessories that *can be worn*. For example 'no jeans or trainers' (sneakers for our international colleagues), is the most common reply. What does this all mean? Most organizations with whom I work have a 'business casual' code but there is an enormous gap in terms of understanding amongst employees as to they can wear to work. Advice tends to be sparse, vague and confusing.

So, time for some clarity, although my first foray into definitions of business casual didn't go too well. The Oxford English Dicitonary[3] offered the following: "designating or characteristic of (a style of) dress which is informal yet smart, esp. smart enough to conform to a particular dress code". No, I don't know what that means either. The Collins English Dictionary[4] suggests: "(*informal*) a style of casual clothing worn by business people at work instead of more formal attire". I define this look as: "business casual is a relaxed but still authoritative look. It should reflect quality, capability, attention to detail, immaculate grooming and a readiness to get to work".

A Framework for Dressing

Deciding what is appropriate means following some 'F's: Formality, Fabric, Finish and Footwear. The degree to which you are more formally or more casually dressed depends on how you interpret each of these categories. So, sit back, relax and enjoy the clarification. Remember, don't be tempted to play the 'yes, but' game. Everything you will read provides you with more choice, so enjoy understanding what they are, rather than looking to find a circumstance in which the approach doesn't apply.

Formality and our Choice of Clothing

Different garments convey different levels of formality when worn. Think three-piece suit versus shorts and t-shirt. Our choice of clothing also *says* different things to the rest of the world, about which we may or may not be aware. The rule is simple, the more clothing we wear, the more formal we are. The less clothing we wear (and more flesh we reveal), the more informal we are. Our clothing conveys different messages. Whether or not that message is appropriate, depends on all of the other considerations outlined above. My other comment is that everything outlined below is relevant for a western world business context. I have deliberately not included in this book the dress code for every part of the world, primarily because it would represent another book all on its own.

The Messages behind a Suit

A very useful resource that has helped me to navigate business casual is based on the work of an international image colleague of mine – Judith Rasband from Conselle L.C and the Institute of Management. In 2000, she developed the Personal/Professional Style Scale[R5] and this framework advises a scale of dressing from tailored to untailored across four key levels. It is to her that I must credit the key messages behind each of level of attire outlined below.

The most formally attired you can be at work is wearing a suit. This is the key design element. We all know (in theory at least), what a suit means. These are matched garments (in other words, two or more garments made from the same fabric and in the same colour), where the fabric is more structured, tailored and smooth. Such garments are usually cool, dark colours, cut to a design with more angles than curves and combined with 'high contrast' (be that a shirt or blouse) and – largely for men – a tie. (Although can I just say that I wear a tie with a shirt to work.) The messages behind these choices of clothing are authority, formality, precision, stability and credibility. Suits are typically viewed as the most formally attired we can be during the day at work. There are some professions for whom a suit is the workplace norm; however, that number has dramatically decreased and the challenge facing most professionals today is answering this question: if it's not a suit; what do I wear to work?

The Messages behind a Jacket

The look that is one level down in terms of formality from the suit is the jacket. The jacket remains the 'power' garment for both men and women and this is because it's (usually) a tailored garment that can convey both influence but also more approachability and more informality than a suit. Endless choice on cut, colours and fabric for the jacket as it can be worn with more informal garments (e.g. casual trousers, jeans) or more formal garments (trousers from a suit but no tie, or combine a jacket with a dress or skirt). Obviously the more formal, structured, tightly woven, and dark and muted in colour the jacket is, then it's a formal garment (like the jacket of a suit). The more relaxed cut, unstructured and loose fabric with bolder pattern and brighter colours it is, then the more informal is the look and message. So, lots of options, but the key garment to wear to convey these messages is a jacket.

The Messages behind a Collar

Well, but if it's not a jacket, what is it, I hear you cry. One level down from a jacket is a collar. A collar is largely an untailored design element of a garment and so is a further foray towards more casual rather than more formal. Think about it. You can find collars on everything from formal shirts to knitwear; from dresses to t-shirts and so on. The messages behind the collar are, therefore, approachability, informality and flexible. It's still influential but less so than either a suit or a jacket, and dependent on your choice of cut, fabric and colour will determine how formal or informal the look becomes.

The Messages behind No Collar

So this is when you wear a tee, knitwear, a collarless shirt, or a dress that is a level of dressing that Conselle L.C^5 describes as collarless. This is the most casually attired at work that we can be and the messages are informal, casual and easy going. The structure of these sorts of garments tends to be more curves (rather than lines and angles), in the construction of a garment, lighter contrast, less tailored, less fitted and not matched with other garments (in the way suit pieces are matched). Interestingly, Conselle L.C^5 also comments at this level about footwear. Wearing 'no collar' can also mean not wearing socks!

So What?

Clothes convey messages to the rest of the world about us whether we like it or not. This has nothing to do with fashion, celebrity or popular culture. The meaning and significance that we draw from clothing has existed for centuries and evolved over the course of them. Any professional who thinks that what they wear to work does not matter and it has no impact on their personal brand and ability to influence others is *at the very best,* extremely naïve. Humans have (and they always will) infer meaning from clothing and we all *always* have choice about what we want to convey to the rest of the world. It's easy to dress 'down', which means that men, for example, could choose to wear a jacket (and/or have a tie to hand) and then be able to reduce the formality of the look as required. It's much harder to 'dress up' (by which I mean to rock up looking very casual and then realize that you've underplayed the formality of the occasion). It's all about being 'appropriate'.

Fabric

Quite frankly thinking about the weight, texture, look and weave of fabric are all enough to have most of us already starting to lose the will to live when considering what to wear. The reality is that most of us really don't spend *any time* thinking about fabric in relation to our clothes. Add to that the notion of colour and most of us have given up (or not even got started) and just reach for what we know and decide not to care. However, when it comes to conveying the right visual signature we should know a little bit about fabric, in order to know what will fit and flatter us best. If you don't want to acquire this information and if you are not already convinced, here's yet another reason to get the support of a qualified image professional who will give the information you need to know and nothing more.

For those of you that do want to know, here are some nuggets. Fabric can be described as light, medium and heavyweight; it can have very smooth or very rough texture and can be very loosely woven or very tightly woven. The rule is this, the more structured and tightly woven the fabric, the more structured it is. So for example, this includes fabrics such as broadcloth, denim and wool organdy. The more relaxed the fabric and more loosely woven it is; the more drape it has, so for example linen, cotton, linen/silk mix. The cut of the fabric determines how formal or informal it is. If we have a straighter, angular body shape then we can easily wear more structured, stiffer fabric. The more curves and contours we have, the more it is essential to wear fabric that can stretch, drape and follow the line of our curves (rather than fighting against them). The weight of the fabric is also important for warmth, as well as structure.

Finish

By this I mean things such as stitching, seam allowance, buttons, hems and linings. These should all be perfect and, as the name suggests, finished off properly. Dropped linings, stretched seams, hanging buttons, worn hems on trousers etc. means that the garment is tired and needs to be either refreshed or retired. We should also beware of garments that are pilling, shiny due to over dry cleaning, worn out (literally), moth holes, torn and so on. Do we want to convey tired, jaded, and worn out? Obviously not. 'It'll do for work' is simply wrong. It's work and we want to inspire and engage others rather than encourage (silently observed) judgment because we look tired, scruffy, unappealing. This is not vanity, narcissism or self-indulgence just to reiterate yet again. This is about leadership. If we look like we don't care about ourselves, it is extremely difficult to convince others that we care about them. Get it right and we notice you; get it wrong and we notice the clothes.

Footwear

The story of footwear is important to our visual signature and it is steeped in history and symbolism. The expression 'down at heel' relates to destitution. Apparently it was first recorded in 1732 by William Darrell in *'A Gentleman Instructed In The Concept Of A Happy Life'*[109] where the phrase 'down at heels' was associated with being impoverished. This was due to being unable to afford to replace worn down heels on shoes. Interestingly, (well that's for you to decide), heels were first worn by men. As far back as the 10th century men wore heels when horse riding and those men who wore heels were associated with owning horses, so the heel became related to the notion of the upper class.

Now, before I get carried away with more detail on the shoe, let's link the simple fact that heels provide height to the notion of influence and 'Executive Presence'.

Malcolm Glick, in his book *'Blink – The Power Of Thinking Without Thinking'*[110] revealed some fascinating research from the United States. The context was implicit bias, but I think it's highly relevant in the context of our 'look'. Gladwell surveyed approximately half the companies on the Fortune 500 list and specifically examined the height of their CEOs. Amongst CEOs of Fortune 500 companies, 58% of this audience were 6 feet or taller. This is 1 metre 82 centimeters for our metric friends amongst us and it compared with an average across the US population of 14.5%. In addition, in general in the United States, there are 3.9% of adult men who are six foot two or taller and this compared with almost a third across Gladwell's survey sample of Fortune 500 CEOs. What I conclude from this is that, quite simply, those of us who are tall are easier to be seen. If we're easier to be seen, it's easier for us to be heard. If it's easier to be heard, then it's easier to influence. Now, for those readers who are perfectly formed in slighter smaller packages, do not despair. Instead, wear heels. Gentlemen, I realize those of you thinking 'easier said than done', then it's really important for you to know how to make the most of your height, and for your clothes to fit you perfectly. Ill-fitting clothes on shorter men will only reinforce the notion of youth or immaturity.

So, let's get back to the shoe for a moment. Essentially for both men and women, the more structure, lines and angles you have in your footwear, the more formal it is. The more relaxed, curved and contoured it is, the more casual it is. Think a premium calf leather monk shoe[121], a premium calf leather brogue[122] for men, for example versus a trainer[123]. Ladies for you – a casual shoe is a ballet shoe[124], a trainer or a flip-flop[125] (thong for our Australian friends – which means something totally different in the US and UK!) and if you prefer to wear a flatter shoe, it needs lines and angles (in other words it needs structure), otherwise it will look too casual. Flat shoes with a suit look horrible for ladies. Now, back to heels. Whilst heels are always better, they need to be comfortable and you need to not look like you're tottering around on stilts.

Know What's Complementary: Fit, Fit, Fit, Fit, Fit

The vast majority of people wear clothes that do not fit them properly. In the United Kingdom, 20% men stated that they have no idea what their real size is and 25% state that they wear clothes that do not fit[8]. As an image professional, my own view is that this figure is extremely conservative. I think the number is much higher, and by the way, I was one of them until I learned some simple rules to help. The first *and in many ways most important thing to know* is that looking good in what you wear is a matter of understanding the shape or line of your body. Your size doesn't matter, but your shape definitely does. Most people don't 'get' that and we live unfortunately in a size-obsessed culture that peddles the illusion of a 'perfect' size (for both men and women). It's all nonsense, extremely unhealthy and divisive. However, what is essential to know is whether you tend to have a body that is relatively straight in shape or whether or not it has curves and contours.

The Reality That We All Just Have To Get Used To

We aren't the size we think we are. Gentlemen, do you think you wear size 36" waist trousers? Ladies, do you think you are a size 12? Here's a fact. Whatever the size written on the label of your clothing, the reality is that it bears almost no resemblance to the reality. Have you ever had the experience of shopping whereby as you move from shop to shop and tried on different garments that are allegedly the same size, but the fit on you are completely different? That's because garments can be labeled the same size, but can be cut in widely different ways. Forget about what you 'think' you are size-wise; and instead focus on getting the perfect fit. Remember, if you look in the mirror and don't like what you see; it's the clothes that are wrong – always. Wearing clothes that fit you properly will always be the most flattering and look most sharp (even when it's a casual environment).

Men and Women and Shapes

Gentlemen, your silhouette can be angular (chest measurement is 7 inches or more than your waist), straight (waist is up to 6 inches smaller than your chest) and clothing should follow the 'line' of your body in order to fit and flatter and whatever you wear, if it fits and flatters then it supports the notion of presence. If your waist measurement is more than your chest measurement then you have a contoured body shape or silhouette.

Ladies, you too have predominantly (yes there are more but let's keep it simple), one of three body shapes - straight, semi-straight or contoured. Look, I could write a book on this specific area alone, but am keeping it simple. Most women tend to carry their 'weight' either in front of them or behind them. Note the word 'weight' is in quotes because I do not mean it in a pejorative sense. If your bust is more than two inches bigger than your hips and you notice that your weight tends to sit on your stomach and chest rather than your bottom, hips and thighs, then you have a straight body shape. Contoured women have curves in all the right places, and can also be 'pear shaped', (so all weight sits on the bottom, hips and thighs). Pear-shaped women have a hip measurement that is more than two inches greater than the bust. It's the same principle as for gentlemen, whatever your size, your clothes need to follow the line of the body in order to fit and flatter.

So how can we tell if our clothing fits us properly? No matter what we wear, here are some incredibly simple tests to discover for ourselves:

FIT TIPS
MEN AND WOMEN
An easy one: if it doesn't sit properly, it doesn't fit properly. Once on, clothes shouldn't need to be adjusted if they fit correctly. When you stand up, sit down, move your arms around, throw some shapes in the canteen, strut down the corridor or anything else you care to do at work, then it's incredibly simple. If your clothes fit you, then they don't need any adjusting during the day.
Horizontal folds anywhere on a garment mean it is too tight.
Vertical folds anywhere on a garment mean that it is

too loose or big.
The shoulder seam on a jacket should sit on your actual shoulder and shouldn't extend past it to 'hang' off you.
Wearing a jacket, lean against a wall to check the placement of the shoulder pad. If when you touch the wall the padding hits it and scrunches up first, it's too big. The pad and shoulder should touch the wall almost simultaneously.
For a jacket, button it and then hug yourself. If you think you're going to burst out (especially at the back), it's too tight. *
Pockets, pleats, lapels, vents should all lie flat and not 'pull' or puff out.
Never have a garment end at the widest part of your silhouette. It adds bulk and weight.
Two fingers should fit in the waistband for comfort on trousers.
Blouse, shirt or dress sleeve lengths should finish at the first joint at the base of the thumb. Avoid excess material at the cuff (indicating the sleeve is too long).

MEN	WOMEN
For gentlemen wearing formal jackets (i.e. as part of a suit or simply a blazer or sports coat to wear with jeans, chinos, cords etc., you can check	The biggest fit issue for women is underwear and specifically getting the bra to fit and sit correctly. Too often the bosom sits too low. A quick and easy

to see the correct length of a jacket by letting your arms hang at your sides. Curl up your hand under the end of the jacket to see if the length of the jacket fits neatly in the crevice. If it hangs above the crevice then the jacket length is too short. If it scrunches up, then the jacket length is too long.	check is this: look at where the bosom sits when wearing a bra and top. It should be level with half way down the arm between the shoulder and elbow.
On a shirt that you intent to wear buttoned up to the top, you should be able to put one finger between your neck and the collar, but not two. Two fingers would suggest that it is too big.	Shirt/blouse/top buttons should never pull or 'gape' in the chest area, otherwise other people will do that at you and it destroys 'presence'.
If you wear a tie, the tip should touch the tops of the belt on your trousers. It's amazing how many senior leaders, politicians and business people that don't know this.	Never have a short sleeve length end at the widest part of your arm. It adds width and bulk.
Formal jacket sleeve length should be shorter	Never have a dress, skirt, boot finish at the widest

than the shirtsleeve length so that you shoot your cuffs properly.	part of your lower leg. All of these fit issues will create the illusion of bulk and width.
Trouser lengths can vary depend on the cut. Narrow cut trousers will sit higher on the shoe. For shorter men, a 'sloping hem' is advised to lengthen the leg.	Trousers should be mid heel of the shoe with which they are worn. Avoid excess material at the bottom of the leg (especially on petite women).
Think 'sometimes, always, never' for the buttons on a jacket. Sometimes you can fasten the top button, always fasten the middle button and never fasten the bottom button.	Avoid 'muffin tops' by making sure the trousers sit on your natural waist and are your right size. Also, check the rise so that it is long enough.
Beware of too much material at the bottom of the trouser, gentlemen. It shouldn't be enough to make a cushion cover. Very easy to get this wrong.	Short skirts and dresses are just a no. I'll admire your legs as much as the next person but that's not where you want people to look if you want to convey presence.

* Editor's note: at time of printing, Daniel Craig was shooting the latest James Bond film where he was

photographed having ripped the back seam of his Tom Ford suit jacket. Whilst I do realize that he is probably leaping about on the tops of high-speed trains fighting nasty villains more often than the rest of us; it remains a good fit tip to know, especially since the rest of us aren't James Bond. And yes, I do concede that some would think he looks even better if the suit was ripped.

Ultimately, the best investment you can make is getting your clothes altered to fit you properly. This is easy, inexpensive and always worth it.

Wearing the Right Colour

I am so over people rolling their eyes when I mention the word 'colour' and what we wear at work. Let's just remove the bias that it is frivolous and pointless and about helping women to wear the right lipstick. Our language and culture is full of the meaning behind colour. Let me direct you back to Barack Obama's experience when he wore a light coloured suit in the White House[11]. Dismiss the importance of colour at your peril. We speak a language of colour. For example, 'seeing red', 'green with envy', 'yellow-bellied' and 'feeling blue'. We emotionally and physically respond to colour[118] and research has shown that, for example, the colour red will elicit a stronger and faster motor response in humans. Everything I have written relates to western business society and that's important to reiterate because different colours do have different connotations.

Writing about colour in a book can be challenging in the absence of pictures, but bear with me. The first and most important thing to say is that when it comes to wearing what works best for you, everything relates to colour worn near your face (because professionally that's where you want people looking, and that's where different colours are in evidence). The best way to know what colours suit you best would be to seek professional advice.

COLOUR	MEANING	HOW TO WEAR IT IN BUSINESS
RED	**Positive:** • Confident, powerful, energetic, driven and determined (which is great!) **Negative:** • Aggressive, brutal and	In a word: accent. In other words, it's great as part of a pattern and also as a tie (which for men will bring colour to your face in the absence of lipstick). Ladies, be thoughtful when you wear a lot of red (e.g. dress etc.) It will make a very

	domineering	bold statement (so think about your goals and objectives).
BLUE	**Positive:** • Confident, loyal, reliable and calm **Negative:** • Boring, too conservative	The metaphorical blue-eyed boy of the colour world in business. It's worn a lot in a professional environment and as a neutral works well for casual shirts, trousers, jeans and knitwear as well as for more formal clothing (e.g. suits).
GREEN	**Positive:** • Fresh, harmonious safe, natural **Negative:** • Envious, selfish, greedy	As part of pattern for shirts and ties (not as a block colour on its own) and also for casual clothing. Don't wear green on your top half with brown on the bottom half. You'll look like a tree.
YELLOW	**Positive:**	Avoid the mustard version of yellow.

	• Optimistic, playful, happy **Negative:** • Immature, unsophisticated, cheap	You will look like 'Coleman's Original'. Yellow is fine in very small doses for men and as an accent colour for a top for women.
ORANGE	**Positive:** • Adventurous, sociable, creative, fun **Negative:** Immature, cheap	If blue is the favoured colour in Western society, then orange is our least favourite colour. In terms of wearing it, my view is never for formal clothing; it's a colour that works best for casual attire. In terms of those people who look best in this colour for casual clothing are those who are natural redheads.
PURPLE	**Positive:** • Creative, high quality, luxurious,	I need to admit a bias. Purple is my favorite colour. As patterns for shirts and ties – divine. As a pale pastel –

	superior	also fabulous. Women have much more choice on variation for this colour for both informal and formal clothing.
	Negative:	
	• Impractical, ostentatious, aloof	

Complete Immaculate Grooming

This is topic that we rarely comment on to others, but we'll silently judge you if you fail here. The point about personal grooming is that the automatic assumption is this topic is a bit like trying to teach you how to look left and right before you cross the road. In other words, it's assumed that we don't need to talk about it because, of course, we all know how to do this and consistently do it.

And yet, let me ask you this: when was the last time you noticed a 'grooming malfunction' in other professionals? I bet it wasn't that long ago. I travel a lot on public transport and let me tell you, dandruff, greasy hair, dirty nails, rough skin, roots showing, scruffy and dirty clothes were on display all over the place. Combine that with bad teeth, poorly applied make-up, a rampant explosion of nose and ear hair all mean that this area simply cannot be assumed. Again, this isn't about vanity or narcissism. Immaculate grooming applies to both the person and the clothes they wear. My view is that if, as a leader, you don't pay attention to this, what it says is that you don't care about yourself. What that then causes me to conclude is that if you don't care about yourself, why on other should I believe that you would care about me? If you want to be known as someone who is reliable, detail-oriented and yet you've not noticed that your clothes are grubby or you've got dandruff, then again, that just doesn't add up. Remember, people with presence are inspiring and engaging, and grubby just doesn't elicit that emotion.

Pay Attention To Details

Accessories

Glasses, jewelry, footwear, handbags are all part of our visual signature. The materials that we use to literally work every day also say something about our personal brand. The bag we use to carry our work 'stuff', pens, folders, our files and our meeting book all count. Our technology (laptops, mobile phones, iPads etc.) all says something about our brand as well. Our challenge is simply this: does it align with what we want the world to 'get' about us? For example, I was working with a senior leader only this week (at time of writing), who wanted to be known for being creative and 'cutting edge'. However, his mobile phone was an old Nokia model that was about 10 years old. Another gentleman wanted to be known for being a 'details man' but hadn't thought what his battered old workbag and chewed top biro might say about him. Also, his glasses were stretched and not sitting properly on his face – as well as being grubby. Are you fed up yet with me saying that this is not about being superficial? It's about being consistent and intentional. The 'look' of a leader is someone who puts consistency, intention and alignment in their visual signature. Remember, we will notice all these things, but never comment. The visual doesn't align with the intent of the brand so instead we silently judge you if you get it wrong.

The Penis Collar Jacket

Well, if ever there was a title for a sub section of a book that you wouldn't imagine reading, I bet it's this one. Highly appropriate for so many reasons, but not least because we have been talking about getting it wrong by not paying attention to the details. As the old adage goes, the devil is in the detail. On those occasions when we do make an error, let me assure you that once noticed, that's all we will focus on when they look at you, and nothing else. We live in the world of the Internet, and our ability to do this well - or not - will be ferociously scrutinized. I need only open my Twitter feed this week as I write to easily find a case to prove my point. There is a Channel Ten television host in Australia called Natarsha Belling. She chose to wear a deep green, long sleeved, formal jacket over a black tee for one of her appearances on screen. Other than a slightly unusual name, nothing so staggering about that is there? And yet, the image (which did not reveal an inappropriate amount of cleavage) attracted more than 110,000 likes on

Facebook and was shared more than 7,000 times[6]. So, what happened? Well, the way that the collar of the jacket was cut prompted some viewers to start commenting on its shape. It looked like a penis. The high contrast between the depth of colour of the jacket and the tee, when set against the pale skin colour meant a clear –albeit unintentional – visual was creating of a phallus. As was made plain on Facebook, "once you see it, you can't un-see it…" And of course, there were a number of wits who started posting captions underneath the screen shot of her choice of outfit which were suitably amusing…"that's a ballsy thing to wear" etc. etc. Of course she didn't mean to do it. The point is, she didn't see it. This is an example of a failure to pay attention to detail and for which Natarsha Belling experienced the consequences. She had unintentionally created a focal point that made her look silly and was very distracting, even when the choices of garments themselves appeared absolutely fine. Every outfit looks different when worn versus when it's on the hanger. (Editor's note: whenever you write about genitals, all language seems to be full of double-entendres and it's a nightmare.)

Signing off on Image

One of the fabulous things about writing is that it is a creative process. On re-reading and endless editing of this chapter, there seemed something so wrong about a chapter on image finishing by talking about the penis. So let's not conclude the conversation about the 'Look' of a leader this way. Let's finish it by saying for the very last time, for all of the reasons outlined and the beginning of this chapter, as a leader you have a chance to convey 'Executive Presence' through how you dress. We have explored all the considerations and choices around how to create and convey the right visual signature through your choice of attire. My invitation to you is to be intentional, consistent and strategic in how you dress. When you do so; you convey presence visually and simply look like a leader.

Chapter Five –
Engage Like a Leader

"The definition of a leader is someone whom people will follow. That means connecting with your people more powerfully than ever before"

Sarah Brummitt

Take a moment to think of leaders whom you admire. They could be leaders within your industry or they could be leaders from another field. They could be people in your organization, or they could be higher profile leaders on a national or international stage. Now consider; what is it that you admire about them? It could be what they have achieved within their business or career to date. It could be their personal accomplishments. It could be the obstacles that they have overcome in order to get where they are today. Whatever the reason, here's the point. You connect with them at an emotional level. I don't necessarily mean that there's general wailing and gnashing of teeth; I mean that how they reach you; how they earn your respect and admiration transcends the rational. They connect with you on an emotional level. I have written repeatedly in this book that leadership is a relationship business. And it is. And that means leadership is about emotion.

What is meant by 'Engage'?

The 'E' in my model is 'Engage'. The simplest definition of 'engage' as a verb that I've found is in the Oxford English Dictionary and it is "to succeed in attracting and keeping somebody's attention and interest"[3]. Well, in terms of leadership I'm strangely underwhelmed by this description. My absolute belief is that this is an incredibly challenging reality facing leaders today. Specifically, what my research determined was that leaders who have Executive Presence and who 'engage' others are quite simply able to do this:

"How you connect with emotion; winning hearts and minds; how you lead with purpose; how you attract, inspire, challenge, support, motivate, develop and influence others."

Now all of this sounds great, doesn't it but who cares? I mean, really, why does this matter and why has this whole area become so relevant in the context of researching Executive Presence? I ask because this is a question posed to me repeatedly by clients. Well, the short answer is to ignore this is to do so at your peril. I have read some horrifying statistics about employee engagement[12] and the numbers are truly frightening:

- 88% of employees don't have passion for their work
- 80% of senior managers are not passionate about their work
- The cost to the US economy of employees who are *not* engaged is more than $500 billion *per year*
- Are you worried yet? If not, read on…
- According to global research from ORC International [13] the United Kingdom rates 18th out of 20 (above only Japan and Hong Kong) in relation to levels of employee engagement.
- The same survey also revealed that the level of engagement in the UK continues to drastically fall.
- In the US, 75% of companies' surveyed[12] are struggling to attract and recruit the best talent needed for their business.
- Two thirds are 'overwhelmed'[12] and 80%[12] would like to work fewer hours.

And here's what the academics would say. The Harvard Service Profit Chain[14] states that organizations that successfully grow and increase their profitability are those who have customers that fully engage with their brand. In other words, these companies have customers who will remain loyal beyond reason and will recommend the organization's brand to others. They will 'advocate' for that brand (do their selling for them). Quite simply, if these customers *love* the experience they have with that brand, then they'll do the selling. All organizations want customers like this. One of my clients is a global car manufacturer that recognizes the importance of driving profitable and successful dealerships isn't just in having great showrooms and fantastic products. If they are to pull ahead in a highly competitive market where margins are very tight, then engaging their people *is by far the most commercially effective way* to do this.

So what does this have to do with Executive Presence and being able to 'Engage' as a leader? It's simple. What determines whether or not a business is able to deliver this kind of customer experience is the degree to which *employees* are engaged with the company for whom they work. Who's responsible for achieving that? The leadership. Being able to, as I put it, connect with emotion; win hearts and minds; how you attract, inspire, challenge, support, motivate, develop and influence others. When you do this, you have an *engaged* workforce. That means they give their 'best selves' to customers, who in turn experience the brand in a way that competitively differentiates that brand from its nearest rivals....and it's so powerful that it can lock them out. Customers exhibit loyalty beyond reason (in other words, they stick with you when you stuff it up). *It's that important.*

What the Research Revealed

Reminding you that one of the questions posed from the survey was:

This section aims to explore views on what Executive Presence is. Put these factors into the order of their importance for being an effective leader, where 1 is the most important and 5 is the least important:

- *How a leader looks*
- *How a leader connects with those they are leading*
- *How a leader behaves*
- *How a leader thinks and makes decisions*
- *How a leader verbally communicates*

Of the five areas above, 55.7% of respondents thought that how a leader connects with those they are leading is most important to demonstrating what Executive Presence is to those around them. Within that response group, 49% of male respondents ranked how a leader connects with those they lead as most important, and this compares with 61% of female respondents. In other words, a higher proportion of females rate this facet of Executive Presence as the most important for leaders to convey.

We then asked the audience to select the top three characteristics that they believe make a leader most compelling. We gave them a long list: ambition, good humour, authenticity, integrity, compassion, recognition, loyalty, power, respect, creativity, humanity, vulnerability, competitiveness and harmony. The 'most voted for' personal characteristic – and by this we mean whether it was ranked first, second or third – was Integrity. 75.3% of votes were cast for this attribute. Authenticity was the second most voted for personal characteristic, with 58.0% of the votes cast for this and Respect was third, with 50.6% of votes cast.

Interestingly, although the entire respondent audience saw integrity as the most important factor, when we explored whether or not there was any gender differences, women put authenticity (the second most important factor overall), as the most important factor. So, if your eyes aren't awash and your head isn't spinning, in simple terms of what all this means when it comes to 'Engage Like A Leader', women rate authenticity as the most important facet of being engaging; whereas for men it's integrity.

For the top three characteristics – integrity, authenticity and respect – every single respondent had at least one of the top three factors in their 'top three' and what this means is that it simply reinforces the importance of these values across the whole community of respondents.

The other angle on importance to think about is that in relation to the 'top three' factors, 99% of respondents said that these were either 'extremely important' or 'important'. What does this mean for leaders? Well, one of the things that I talk often about is the need to be clear on your personal brand – which is defined by key values or characteristics that you want the world to consistently 'get' about you. Therefore, what my research shows is that whatever your personal brand values are (and it doesn't matter *what* they are), the piece that is critical is that *if* that value is true for you, then that is what people around you will engage with. Your brand values need to be truthful for you because that's how people will connect with you and that's how you as a leader will be able to engage with them.

Why is Integrity so Important to Convey for Leaders who have Executive Presence?

It strikes me that integrity has been all too easily assumed to exist where, in fact, the case to the contrary has become overwhelming. Across not only the business community, but also other facets of our society such as sports, politics, show business and – dare I say it – religion, to name but a few, the examples of a lack of integrity are everywhere. The size and shape of their misdemeanours – well I'll leave that to you to categorize – but make no mistake, integrity is in short supply in some quarters and to continue to assume that is a given is naïve at best and dangerous at worst.

Enron[20] represented one of the most spectacular falls from grace as the dot.com bubble finally burst at the start of the new millennium. In 2001, the company filed for Chapter 11 bankruptcy in the US having been lauded for its extraordinary commercial success a few short years earlier. Its shares reached an all-time high in August 2000, but by November 2001 the stock was downgraded to 'junk bond' status. Ken Lay and Jeffrey Killing (former CEO and Chairman) were found guilty of eye-watering securities and accounting fraud plus conspiracy. Their lies, deceit and treachery were staggering. And they are not alone in the business world.

Dennis Kozlowski and Mark Swartz of Tyco were found guilty of misappropriating corporate funds, tax fraud and tax evasion.

I'll just say the words 'Lehman Brothers', a 158 year old investment bank that collapsed on September 15th 2008 by filing for Chapter 11 bankruptcy in the US with the largest filing in US history of $639 billion of assets, to remind you of what happened to that particular organization.[26]

Martha Stewart – a US icon and bastion of home-making was convicted in 2004 of obstructing justice and lying to investigators in relation to an insider trading enquiry. Stewart was listed by Forbes[21] as Number 377 of The 400 Richest Americans, with a net worth of over $970M.

Lord John Browne was one of the most successful business leaders in the UK and Chief Executive of

British Petroleum (BP), who was forced to step down after lying under oath about his private life[22].

David Edmondson was the Chief Executive of Radio Shack who falsified his resume by claiming that he had two college degrees when, in fact, he had none.[23]

And the list goes on. Let's switch gears - and forgive the pun. One of the most astoundingly sad and shocking sporting heroes who fell from grace was Lance Armstrong. A two-time cancer survivor (that is definitely true), fundraiser extraordinaire and seven-time winner of the Tour de France was revealed to be a dope-taking cheat, a bully, a liar and an extreme manipulator. Stripped of his titles, forced to step away from his charitable foundation, Armstrong, to this day, appears defiant, unrepentant and determined to defend himself.[24]

And cycling isn't the only sport that has suffered from the taint of cheating. As long ago as the mid-1990s, the supposed doyen of good sportsmanship, the sport of cricket became tainted by corruption. Hanse Cronje[33] was a brilliant cricket captain. He led South Africa to 42 victories from 53 tests and inspired 138 one-day international successes. Cronje was widely acknowledged as a brilliant, inspirational captain for his country. In 2000 he was found guilty of taking bribes[34] to provide insider information for bookies. His subsequent fall from grace and premature death in

2002 marked a very sad and sorry end to what was an outstanding cricketer, but deeply flawed man.

Moving away from sports, let's go to the world of entertainment. Jimmy Savile[25] was a BBC Television presenter in the United Kingdom and a charity fundraiser who presented 'Jim'll Fix It'[145]. This programme was a peak-time, family show geared towards children writing to him to ask for his help to achieve a wish. He died in October 2011, but since his death, it has emerged that he abused hundreds of children and may be one of the most prolific paedophiles in British history.

The Catholic Church in the United Kingdom has an organization called the National Catholic Safeguarding Commission who reported that more than 50 'de-frockings' have occurred in the last decade since new guidelines were introduced[27]. The UK is not the only country that has reported on this issue for The Catholic Church. I know religion is a difficult topic and I am very conscious the Catholic faith is not the only faith that has been tinged by the evil of child abuse.

In the world of politics, Senator John Edwards was on the Democratic Vice President campaign ticket in the 1990s, but it subsequently transpired that he had cheated on his wife who was dying from cancer[28]. After his failed presidential campaign, Edwards was later tried on charges of violating campaign finance law.[29] And on the topic of politicians, let's just cast our minds back to the behaviour of what was the world's most powerful man in the 1990s, President Bill Clinton, and his involvement with Monica Lewinsky, which threw his second presidency into disarray and caused him to be impeached as a result. A side note – she was vilified for her behaviour; he survived the impeachment hearing and still remains a respected leader on the world stage. How does that work?

The list goes on and on and it's easy to get very depressed. So let's stop and turn to a much more interesting question.

How does a Leader 'Do' Integrity?

John Wooden was an American college basketball coach who was quite simply an *astounding* coach and leader. He was awarded Coach of the Year six times, won a record ten national championships over 12 years in charge of the UCLA, enjoyed an 88 game winning streak and was also the first person to be inducted to the Basketball Hall of Fame as both as a player and a coach. Why am I talking about him? Because it strikes me that when it comes to the notion of 'integrity', it is a quote credited to him that speaks to much of what we're talking about in leaders who have 'Executive Presence'. Wooden said, "The true test of a man's character is what he does when no one is watching". And of course, this premise sits completely at odds with the behaviour of the long list of people mentioned above.

So integrity is about consistency between what is said and what is done; the notion of 'doing the right thing', no matter what. It's also about taking responsibility; making the difficult decisions; knowing the difference between right and wrong; being utterly, unswervingly trustworthy. Michael Hyatt wrote in a fabulous blog entitled 'Ten Mistakes That Leaders Should Avoid At All Costs'[30] that *"there are many things you can lack and still steer clear of danger. Integrity isn't one of them. Establish a set of sound ethics policies, integrate them into all business processes, communicate them broadly to all employees, and make clear that you will not tolerate any deviation from any of them. Then live by them".*[30]

How does a Leader *Communicate* Purpose?

At the top of this chapter I said that the definition of a leader is someone whom people choose to follow. John Baldoni in his book *Lead With Purpose* [31] quotes an army general who says *"I don't think you can hit purpose enough as a senior leader. It is one of those things that can be under communicated by an order of magnitude. You cannot oversell, over pronounce, "Here's why we're here".*

To his point, I cannot write about the concept of communicating integrity and communicating the notion of purpose without talking about the work of an academic that I am *obsessed with*. Simon Sinek, in his book *Start With Why*[32] has decoded what's different about those individuals and companies who inspire and those who do not. Sinek defined inspiring leaders and companies as those which have the most loyal employees, the most loyal customers, can charge a premium if they want to, are innovative and **most importantly** are not just 'here one minute; gone the next'. Sinek says that regardless of the industry, every single one of these leaders and organizations that are inspirational, all think, act, behave and communicate in **exactly the same way,** and it is the complete opposite to everyone else.

Start With Why[32] has at its heart a simple concept called the Golden Circle. I know this sounds rude, but bear with me. Every single organization on the planet knows *what* they do. In other words, they know all about – and indeed are the experts - on the products they sell and the services they offer. Some of these businesses know *how* they do it. In other words, how a business operates successfully is through its differentiating value proposition, or its proprietary technology or lean process. These are just illustrative examples; the point being the 'how' is how you are special or different when compared to everyone else in your market. So, here's the best part. What Sinek[32] found was that there were a very small number of leaders and a very small number of organizations that were able to articulate *why* they do what they do.

So Sinek uses the concept of three concentric circles to demonstrate his point. On the 'inside' circle is the 'why', the middle circle is the 'how' and the outer circle is the 'what'.

And before we all leap to the obvious answer – that being to make money – then just hold your horses. Sinek says that making money is a result, but *it is not your purpose.* Your purpose is your reason for existence as a company. It's your beliefs or your cause. It could be your calling. It's very simply the reason why your company exists at all. The sceptics amongst you might be wondering 'who cares'? But here's the thing. Whatever your business is – as a leader let's be honest: do we really need another business of whatever it is that you do? I mean, really? There's plenty of choice out there, wouldn't you say? You're no different are you?

The consequence of not 'starting with why' is that the way leaders think, act and communicate is from the outside to the inside of the Golden Circle[32]. We start by talking about the clearest thing (the *what)* and then finish with the most opaque thing (the *why)*. Oh and by the way, we still expect our customers to buy from us. Sinek found that this was fundamentally the way that inspirational leaders and organizations think, act and communicate. Instead, what they do is the complete opposite: they communicate from the 'inside' of the Golden Circle outwards. In other words, they start with *why.*

Sinek refers to Apple as one example of this concept in powerful action. Remembering, of course, that Apple is just a corporate structure like any other of the multitude of corporate structures in the west coast of the US. They have access to the same resources, same talent and same agencies as all of their competition. However, they have become a giant within their industry. So, how come? Well, if Apple communicated in the same way as everyone else, a piece of communication would sound like this: *"We make great computers. They're beautifully designed, easy to use and really, really clever. Want to buy one?"* How inspiring does this sound? The answer is not so much. It's all right, but it doesn't make the eyes dance does it? However, the late Steve Jobs didn't communicate in this way. He wanted to change the world (and boy did he ever). His communication might sound something like this *"at Apple we believe in challenging the status quo. We believe in pushing the boundaries of what we do by thinking differently. How we do that is by making products that are beautifully designed and user-friendly. What we produce are laptops, iPhones and iPads".* The point is, that reads differently, it sounds different and, of course, it is different. It is far more inspiring and engaging. However, because Apple has defined itself by its cause/belief or why – that's why it's succeeded where others have failed.

Sinek also commented that we are all comfortable with the idea that Apple sells more than computers. They sell tablets, phones, mp3 players and DVRs. However, they weren't the first company to do this. Dell Computers made a foray into the arena a number of years ago, but came up against one important hitch – they failed. Dell launched into the market their own version of an mp3 player and PDA. But they failed to inspire and excite the audience.

In other words, if we are to inspire and engage others, transform our business and succeed in the long term; it is *essential* that we know *why* we're doing what we're doing and to continually communicate that to our employees, customers and suppliers alike. If we don't know why we do what we do; why would anyone else?

My 'why' is simply that I believe that professional men and women have an eye-watering amount of potential. How my business is all about helping them to tap into more of that potential to achieve whatever they want from they want from their career. How I do that is by creating and delivering a wide range of group and 1:1 solutions that focus on exquisite influencing skills.

What's your 'why'?

How does a Leader 'Do' Authenticity?

Winning hearts and minds means getting 'real'. It means conveying vulnerability and authenticity like never before as a leader and I refer here to another brilliant academic to make the case. Brené Brown[35] in her book *Daring Greatly: How the Courage to Be Vulnerable Transforms the Way We Live, Love, Parent, and Lead* and is a superb, ground-breaking take on the notion of vulnerability. In a leadership context, her premise is simple – vulnerability is a sign of strength, not weakness.

Here's how it works. Let's compare two different contexts. If as a leader our mind-set is 'never let your guard down', what is created in a climate where only perfection is tolerated? If we operate from a place that says 'don't show any weakness' what happens is that consequently, our people will not ask for help because they perceive this to be viewed badly. They will make mistakes and then hide them from us and they will become ever more disengaged from their working environment. Brown calls this 'disingenuous leadership'.

Contrast this with a mind-set that says, as a leader we have the courage to be ourselves – for all that is good, bad and indifferent about being ourselves. The consequence of this approach is that different individual strengths are utilised and as a result our people develop, ask for help when they need it, own up to their mistakes and are willing to fix them, have a level of connection and engagement to the business that makes them want to give their 'best selves' at work.

I have a client who is a service leader. He is bright, clever, honest and also impatient, irritable and stressed. When he gets it wrong he knows it. He upsets people and can make them cry. Our journey over the last year has been about helping him understand the impact of how his presence can create real highs and lows within his organization. Being authentic doesn't mean 'just take me as I am and too bad if you don't like it'. It's about being honest enough to admit our frailties and finding different ways to cope and communicate when our frailties catch up with us. He has transformed the engagement of his people through focusing on being vulnerable and developing his professional and personal skills to become simply must more effective (and engaging!) as a leader.

How does a Leader *Communicate* Vulnerability?

Let's talk practical strategies and skills and I am drawn back to Brown's book.[35] To be clear, her book was based on the following fundamental assumptions:

- Making connections with others is the basis of life.
- We don't make connection because we feel we are not good enough. This causes shame.
- To make real connection we have to have a **strong sense of worthiness** and be **willing to be vulnerable.**
- If you look at these three points, it's fair to suggest that relates to our non-verbal communication. In other words:
- Successful body language is about making powerful connections.
- We have unsuccessful body language when we have shame and feel vulnerable that we are not good enough.
- To make real connection we have to be willing to have **authentic body language** and **believe we are worthy**.

So, in terms of what we need to say, as leaders we need to learn to say more often:

- I don't know
- I need help
- I disagree—can we talk about it?
- It didn't work, but I learned a lot
- Can you teach me how to do this?
- I played a part in that
- I accept responsibility for that
- Let's move on
- I'm sorry

- Thank you.

Brené Brown also shares some advice about how to give feedback to others. This is an important topic for leaders. In fact, vulnerability is especially important when giving feedback to others, because it puts you in a mindset of "this is a problem for us to address" versus "you just need to get your act together". Examples include:

- I'm ready to sit next to you rather than across from you.
- I'm willing to put the problem in front of us rather than between us.
- I'm ready to listen, ask questions, and accept that I may not fully understand the issue.
- I recognize your strengths and how you can use them to address your challenges.
- I'm willing to own my part.
- I can model the vulnerability and openness that I expect to see from you.
- Put the problem in front of us rather than between us

I have another client who (so far) has made my year. He began a team meeting (which I was attending to observe his communication skills in action). When we first met he was hostile, passive aggressive and quite closed. We had four sessions followed by a break. He then contacted me to ask to get together this year for four more sessions. Our first appointment was arranged with me attending his senior leadership meeting as an external observer. He began (and I had no idea he was going to do this), by saying that he'd been totally resistant to being coached and had told me (and he had at our very first meeting), that it was all a waste of his time. When I offered him the option of immediately stopping, he was extremely surprised and only insisted that we continue in order to not give me what he thought I wanted! Then he began to realize that he needed help and over the intervening six months his wife and family had passed comment on things that started to connect with our conversations. He said he was humbled and ashamed of his approach and so grateful for another opportunity to become a better leader. Let me tell you, all of us sat there with our mouths open, but he did more in that one moment to engage, inspire and delight his people through his vulnerability than anything over the last two years. More than one of us had something in our eye at that moment, let me tell you.

How does a Leader 'Do' Respect?

Another fabulous resource (look I'll throw a lot at you; you decide what you want to peruse) is by The Arbinger Institute. They wrote a super book called 'Leadership And Self Deception'[146]. The simple, but profound premise is that we may just all be deluding ourselves. We don't like to think that we are not respectful of others, and yet we are – very regularly.

We don't like to think that we may not consider the views and opinions and feelings of others, and yet we don't – very often. Here are some of my questions for leaders that reveal the culture of their organization and the propensity to communicate disrespectfully to others. By the way, culture is what we create and condone, and it's our responsibility. It's not a vague concept that is removed from us. Some of the questions I am curious about include:

- Are you ever late to conference calls or meetings?
- Is it acceptable to use technology whilst talking to someone else?
- Do you leave meetings/calls earlier than promised due to a (real) business emergency? Or change plans at the last minute?
- Do you 'no show' or cancel meetings/events?
- Do you not listen fully to others on occasion?
- Do you interrupt others whilst they are talking, presenting etc.?
- Do you spend less than 20% of your time genuinely appreciating and thanking others?
- Is the majority of your total communication electronic? (Text, email, etc.)
- Do you talk about your own expertise/experiences a lot?
- Do you think that you're the best at most things?
- Do you think that you are rarely wrong?
- Do you rarely admit to others that you were wrong?
- Do you rarely apologize?

- Do you rarely seek feedback on your performance from others (whether or not they are at the same 'peer' level as you?)?

Frankly, the list goes on and on. However, if we've answered 'yes' to even one of those questions then the chances are we've been disrespectful as leaders. Being respectful begins with a genuine self-awareness of what you do at the moment. You'll also notice that different behaviours can communicate more than one facet of 'engaging' as a leader. Beyond that all I can say is 'read on'. There is plenty in this chapter and across a number of chapters that can help.

How Does A Leader 'Do' Humility?

In May 2014, the Senior Vice President of People Operations for Google was quoted in The Times[154] as saying that one of his critical traits for new hires was humility. Lazlo Bock (great name), defined humility not just in terms of allowing others to contribute, but "it's also intellectual humility. Without humility, you are unable to learn". Research from the Administrative Science Quarterly in January2014[155] revealed that leaders who convey humility achieve greater levels of employee engagement and improved job performance than leaders who did not. Our research reveals that humility is part of Executive Presence and so naturally we were curious to understand how to 'do' humility. In so doing, you will see a thread running from some of the other areas of Executive Presence, so the good news is that you can kill more than two birds with one stone – as it were.

- Admit mistakes. Operating from the delusion that you don't make any is in itself a mistake. Thinking that if you admit to a mistake then this will be viewed as weak is, in itself, a mistake. Personal story – I used to work for someone who in five years never owned up to making a mistake, and yet spent an inordinate amount of time 'giving feedback' on other people. No wonder morale went through the floor and lots of great people left. The company is still struggling. By admitting mistakes and be willing to own up to them helps build trust and models the behavior we want to see our people exhibit themselves. It also creates an opportunity for it to become a 'teachable moment'. Making your mistakes part of your own personal story encourages others to do the same – admitting they are not perfect – only reinforces our perception of being human.
- Take personal risks for the greater good.
- Focus on the needs of others. Research shows that when leaders demonstrate that they are focused on the needs of others – whether it is in a large, strategic context (e.g. we are going to invest to protect and grow jobs), or in a day-to-day context (the most impactful of which is always 1:1 conversations, whether ad hoc or planned).
- Be willing to say 'I don't know'. My sense is that this is hard for leaders who value control, but the

reality is, of course, that we cannot know all the answers.

- Seek feedback – Chairmanship skills 101 say that seeking the input of others to a discussion or decision is *essential* to getting the best from others. Who on earth wants to work for someone who doesn't ask for his or her input? Or doesn't value their input? Or who simply dismisses it? This is not about being excruciatingly inclusive; it's about genuinely seeking the opinions of others in order to make the best possible decision for the business.

- Take time outs – because if we do not make time to connect with ourselves and our perceptions, emotions and opinions in relation to work, then how can we be realistic about how we relate and connect with others around us? Wherever we go; there we are.

How does a Leader 'Do' Poise?

I guess it's useful to start by asking ourselves how much poise we have at the moment. President Ronald Regan was renown for sound bites – once said: 'I have learned that one of the most important rules in politics is poise. This means looking like an owl after you have behaved like a jackass'[74]. Consider this for a moment. Are you someone who can:

- Laugh at yourself when the joke is on you?
- Remain positive when things start to go wrong?

- Stay calm in a crisis?
- Take feedback/criticism without becoming very emotional?

The chances are that if you've answered 'yes' to these questions, then you have a fair amount of poise already – which is great. The way to develop poise is to focus on those things that destroy it. So, anger, frustration, tiredness are all examples. Poise starts from within. If our internal world is a kaleidoscope of emotions that are hurtling around, bubbling out, working to exhaust, excite and exercise us, then let's face it, poise will be difficult. I am very aware that writing about our 'internal world' can be a bit – well, challenging – for some of us. However, we need to pay attention to our beliefs and operating assumptions because that drives what we tell the world – verbally and non-verbally, as well as consciously and sub-consciously. What does that mean?

- Make time to pause and be very still, every single day. No phones, emails, calls, texts or other distractions. Stop, focus on breathing, if possible simply close your eyes for a couple of minutes and notice your own body.
- Let go of the past. Someone once said to me "'the past is a different country". How gloriously true that is. When we keep going back to points or places in our past that elicit really strong, negative emotions then it does nothing good for our emotional wellbeing – and sense of poise.

- Learn to stay present. Having said that the past has the capability to not be good for us, equally so can the future. Becoming very present is part of evolving poise.
- Pay attention to what we call 'internal dialogue'. That's our inner voice that is constantly chirruping away with thoughts. What do we say to ourselves? Especially when times are challenging? If our conversations with ourselves are negative, critical, cruel, spiteful and intolerant then *no wonder* that we might struggle to convey poise.
- Learn to laugh often. Laughing is quite simply good for the soul. We have to find a way to feel lighter, freer and quite simply happy. Even if it's only for moments.
- Find a stronger sense of gratitude. People who are poised are happier and part of that is finding things to be grateful for – every day. It doesn't always have to be big, heavy things either. A great cup of coffee, a compliment, a conversation with a friend, a great view. Anything for which we can genuinely relish the moment.

Now then, there are many things we can do with our bodies to convey poise (our walk, posture, way we hold our head, eye contact etc.). I've not expanded on that here – check out what we can do to manage our body in the 'Act' chapter. A number of strategies will support demonstrating poise. I wanted here to answer the question at a deeper, internal level. Why? Because get this right; and all of the external manifestations of poise become *so much easier.*

How does a Leader 'Do' Confidence?

The phrase 'fake it until you make it' is well known. Amy Cuddy, an Associate Harvard professor explains in her brilliant Ted talk[119] how we can go much further than faking it. Our body operates in a way where we can 'fake it until we become it'. Cuddy reveals that there are plenty of things that we can do to organize our body so that we communicate (and become) more confident – more of that in the 'Act' chapter as well. However, here I'd like to comment on our 'internal world'. Our internal word drives how we represent ourselves to the external world. In many ways it's that simple. I am passionate about the concept of the most important relationship to get right isn't with our boss, our colleagues, our team. It's not even with our partners or children. It's actually the relationship we have with ourselves. Wherever we go, there we are. We can't get all these other relationships right if we don't have a great relationship with our self. Now, I'm not straying too much into the psychotherapy field, save to say that it's *essential.* There are so many signs and ways in which we let the world know what we've been saying to ourselves and how we feel about ourselves. For example, my very first question whenever I work with any client is very simple: 'how are you'? It's casual, often asked as we're meeting, getting coffee and getting settled and definitely long before we jump into the session. It's not just what is said; it's *how it's said* that I find so revealing. What am I hearing? Confidence? Certainty? Excitement? Happiness? Or am I hearing doubt? Fear? Scepticism?

So, in the context of how as leaders we 'do' confidence, what I am curious about is our internal dialogue. Many things we can do to convey confidence in terms of our verbal and non-verbal behavior (see both of those chapters!) However, here I want to talk about what do we say to ourselves most of the time? I'm particularly interested in what we say to ourselves when in a high-pressure situation? Do we say things like 'don't stuff this up'; 'you've no right to be here'; 'I'm really nervous' etc.? Let's just think about this for a moment. How helpful is that? Not remotely of course. However, what it does is heighten our anxiety and increase our nerves. So, let's instead focus on (a) breathing deeply – never to be underestimated as a strategy and (b) focus on saying things which are true and which we can genuinely believe. For example: 'I have prepared for this session' or 'I know this topic' or 'my opinion is important to hear' or whatever the words or phrases are that you can own, believe and repeat in those moments right before the spotlight turns to you.

In addition, it is *essential* to make time to reflect on your success and achievements. Making time to do this and, as my very first boss said, investigate success with even more curiosity than we investigate failure.

When we do so; there is liquid gold to be mined and replicated to enhance our effectiveness and the effectiveness of others.

How does a Leader 'Do' Credibility?

Credibility builds trust. It also takes time. If you have read this entire chapter then you'll already know that a number of the strategies that have been mentioned so far are not mutually exclusive. In other words, what we might 'do' to convey credibility might also apply to authenticity and so on. My point is that there are not singular strategies for different traits of 'engage' to convey Executive Presence. There are multiple strategies that can convey a number of different traits to engage others. So how can leaders convey credibility? Below are some simple (but don't be fooled) strategies that genuinely make a difference:

- What we say and what we do is the same thing. Our people aren't idiots. If we say one thing and do another, then we can forget being seen as credible. For example, many organizations talk about their corporate values. These can be found on walls, corporate collateral, in the signatures of peoples' emails and even in the visitors' loos. However, that doesn't mean anything if that's all that happens. It is how those values are demonstrated through daily behaviours. That's what counts. If what we profess to 'value' and then the way in which we subsequently treat our people are not aligned, then we're not believed and we're simply not credible.

- We are consistent. I have talked elsewhere in this chapter about the 'manager on meds' scenario. What I mean by that simply is that part of our survival mechanism is our ability to gauge the mood/approach/style of others. If we are charming, polite and upbeat one day and then rude, aggressive and negative the next then we are not consistent and that destroys trust. It also means we're simply not credible. The 'little' things that aren't really 'little' always strike me. For example, I had a client who always went 'yeah, yeah, yeah' repeatedly and what he hadn't realized was that it conveyed a sense of 'I know all this and I know everything' to his team. As a behaviour, it contradicted with the value of 'humility'.
- We take responsibility. By that I mean for when we get it wrong as much as when we get it right. Otherwise we run the risk of always 'being right' or 'being perfect' and even if we think we are, no one else does.
- Being seen as an expert (or at least competent) in an area of domain expertise is another way of building credibility. If we are genuinely an expert in certain areas, or if we have particular skills that are stronger than most, then for some, this will represent a powerful means by which to engage others. Quite simply, what we're good at, others value.
- We take action. Leaders who are 'all talk' aren't credible. We have to 'do' as well as 'say'. My first

sales leader said to me 'I will never ask you to do what I wouldn't do myself'. Being willing to act and being willing to lead from the front all convey credibility and engage others.

How does a Leader Do Self-Awareness?

Here we enter the fabulous world of emotional intelligence. Daniel Goleman's book[147] is another brilliant resource to add to your library. I am grateful to Psychology Today[148] for some clarity on a definition. Specifically emotional intelligence is generally said to include three skills:

1. Emotional awareness, including the ability to identify your own emotions and those of others.
2. The ability to harness emotions and apply them to tasks such as thinking and problem solving.
3. The ability to manage emotions, including the ability to regulate your own emotions, and the ability to cheer up or calm down another person.

And it's not easy. EQ rather than IQ is how we, as leaders, are going to stand any chance of inspiring, engaging, motivating and delighting others. I worked for someone who was - and still is - the most intelligent person I have ever met. However their EQ was – and still is - also the lowest. As a result they became the most demoralizing, negative, soul-sapping, confidence draining, uninspiring boss to work for. They lost talented people at every turn – and yet it was never their 'fault'. This person genuinely believed that they were the best at any task, skill, and activity within the business and that's simply naïve. And they didn't realize their impact on others. Whether it's in terms of 'chemistry' between two individuals or whether it's within an interaction, leaders with Executive Presence who have high emotional intelligence are very aware of when we're talking too much/little; being perceived as funny/unfunny; making valuable contributions to a meeting/talking a load of nonsense – all of these things we are aware of *in the moment*. As always, the quality of our communication is in the response it elicits.

I think having self-awareness also means having a relentless curiosity in understanding ourselves. Any opportunity to complete psychometric testing, get professional coaching, mentoring, training is simply too good an opportunity to pass up. But it's also in the curiosity of genuinely seeking feedback from others. A delegate described me this week on a workshop as 'flamboyant'. I was amazed!

How does a Leader Win Hearts and Minds?

Well, effectively our ability to connect with people at an emotional level is essential. Being emotionally intelligent has to be the place to start. Being human, being honest, authentically praising others, telling inspiring stories, living your values, being vulnerable are all places to start – as indeed many of the things I talk about in this very chapter. Effectively there are *so many things that we can do* to win hearts and minds is the short answer to that question, and there are a host of practical tips and techniques for our verbal communication in the 'Resonate' chapter that will help. It's well worth a read.

How does a Leader Challenge and Support Their People?

Our challenge as leaders is to get this right. Leaders who convey Executive Presence are always looking for ways to develop and extend the talents and capabilities of their people and balance the two paradigms that allow this to happen. Those paradigms are challenge and support. There is a fantastic model based on the work of Nevitt Sandford[149] that reveals four possibilities in terms of how we, as leaders, can get it right (but often wrong).

Low Challenge and Low Support: This drives apathy. Our people have extremely low expectations, low achievement, low standards, are isolated, demoralized and loathe new initiatives. So nothing good there then.

Low Challenge and High Support: This drives under achievement. Complacency, frustration, more low achievement, low expectations, a lack of knowledge and low standards.

High Challenge and Low Support: This drives anxiety. There are high expectations, inconsistent achievement, variable standards, and a culture of blame, fear of failure, low morale and divisive competition.

High Challenge and High Support: This drives empowerment. There is a culture of high expectations, high achievement, high standards, a tolerance of making mistakes, taking risks, a willingness to embrace change and a tolerance of making mistakes.

Now then, that all sounds great, doesn't it? Everything about how you demonstrate leadership through Executive Presence will either drive high challenge or high support – or – it won't. Our challenge as leaders is to start this conversation with our people and be curious about how our teams and our people want/need to be challenged and how they want/need to be supported.

Do we:

- Understand our people's motivations for work?

- Identify what they want to do in terms of their career?
- Know the things that drive them crazy? (Large or small)
- Know how they like to be appreciated? Rewarded?
- Give regular feedback (both positive and developmental)?
- Provide clarity in our communications?
- Drive responsibility and accountability through the team?
- Listen to them?
- Make time for them?

I have the privilege of working with a sales leader in retail who can genuinely say 'yes' to all the questions above. However, if the rest of us can't, then we have work to do to engage our people. And engaged workforces drives engagement with our customers, our suppliers, and our partners and enables any commercial metric that we care about to be met. It's what enables our business to stand out ahead of our competition and win. It's *that important.* How we engage our people through our Executive Presence creates the culture that determines our success. It's not the responsibility of 'the business' or 'the brand' or 'they' or 'the powers that be' or 'management' or any other euphemistic term. It's down to us as individuals and leaders.

Chapter Six –
Act Like a Leader

"The war for talent is raging. If leaders fail to engage both head and heart, then the best talent will find organizations that do"

Sarah Brummitt

What is Meant by 'Act'?

What the survey revealed that 'Act' meant was: 'how you behave; your non-verbal communication; how you strategize with your physical presence; using your body to support not subtract from your verbal message'. The word 'act' requires some more clarity because initially, I was hesitant to use this word. You'll see why in a moment. The Oxford English Dictionary[3] defines 'act' as either 'to take action; do something' or, 'fulfill the function or serve the purpose of', or, 'to take effect'. Well, that all makes sense of course. However, here's what the word act *does not* mean: 'to behave so as to *appear* to be; to *pretend* to be'. Acting like a leader ***does not mean pretending.*** This is not fake or false or fiction. It needs to be 100% authentic and ***real.***

What We Asked

Reminding you that one of the questions posed from the survey was:

This section aims to explore views on what Executive Presence is. Put these factors into the order of their importance for being an effective leader, where 1 is the most important and 5 is the least important:

- *How a leader looks*
- *How a leader connects with those they are leading*
- *How a leader behaves*
- *How a leader thinks and makes decisions*
- *How a leader verbally communicates*

How a leader behaves (you will note that I changed the word to 'behave' from 'act') was deemed by the audience to be the second most important factor in being an effective leader.

We then asked about specific behaviours that the respondents believed that successful leaders demonstrated most. Here, it was impossible (without damaging the integrity of the survey structure), to distinguish verbal and non-verbal communication, so we structured the question as follows:

Please indicate the extent to which you believe successful leaders demonstrate the following behaviours:

- *They have clear, concise communication*
- *They use positive body language (e.g. smile, nod)*
- *They maintain good eye contact*
- *They use gestures highly effectively*
- *They appear in control at all times*
- *They put others at ease*
- *They listen*
- *They reassure*
- *They admit when they are wrong*
- *They always focus on the positive, even when things are going wrong*

This section aimed to draw out your views on how successful leaders behave.

The narrative structure for answering the questions was:

- *Strongly agree*
- *Agree*
- *Neither agree nor disagree*
- *Slightly disagree*
- *Strongly disagree*

What The Research Revealed

86.4% of the survey respondents *strongly agreed* that clear, concise communication was important in being a successful leader. However, I am not at all surprised by the second most important behavior – and that's non-verbal. It is 'listening'. 79.0% of respondents strongly agreed that this was an important behaviour for being successful. From the behaviours below we then asked which of these is the *single most important* behaviour for being successful as a leader.

- *They have clear, concise communication*
- *They use positive body language (e.g. smile, nod)*
- *They maintain good eye contact*
- *They use gestures highly effectively*
- *They appear in control at all times*
- *They put others at ease*
- *They listen*
- *They reassure*
- *They admit when they are wrong*
- *They always focus on the positive, even when things are going wrong*

39.8% of respondents stated that leaders have clear, concise communication. 25% stated that leaders listen, 17.0% stated that leaders appear in control at all times and then a large gap to 10.2% who chose the behavior of 'put others at ease', 4.5% picked the behaviour of leaders needing to always focus on the positive, even when things are going wrong and finally, using highly effective gestures.

Let me go back to 'listening' if I may. Of those respondents who chose 'listening' as the single most important behavior, there was a noticeable gender difference. Of the 75% of the respondents who chose 'listening', 75% were women. So, at the risk or reinforcing something that we might already know, as a leader, if you want to be persuasive, engaging and influential to a female audience, then 'listening' is the number one behavior that you need to authentically demonstrate.

Different Perspectives Depending on Role Level

It is worthy to note that 18.5% of the respondents disagreed or strongly disagreed that 'always focusing on the positive, even when things are going wrong' is a behaviour that contributes to success as a leader. This is the only area in the whole of the survey where a section of respondents strongly disagreed with anything. The conclusion has to be that this reinforces the importance of integrity as a leader, and specifically that people always want the truth – whether it's good, bad or indifferent. Digging in to this a little further, when you analyze the different job roles in relation to this question, 'focus on the positive, even when things are going wrong' was rated as the most important behavior by Board Level Executives, Business

Owners and Team Members, (so the two ends of the spectrum), but not from any of the management tiers.

'Appearing in control of things at all time' was viewed as an important behavior by all functional levels apart from front line supervisors who all considered 'listening' as the most important behaviour for being a successful leader.

Interestingly enough, it was only respondents who were business owners who identified that 'admitting they were wrong' was an important behavior for leaders. Isn't that fascinating? So, you could argue that it is less desirable to be seen to be wrong in a corporate environment. This must put a real challenge on integrity and authenticity for leaders from time to time, don't you think?

Listening And Leadership

Basically, we suck at listening. D.A. Benton's book 'When Lions Don't Need To Roar'[15] suggests that leaders hear less than 30% of what is said. Let's just stop and think about that for a moment. We hear less than one in every three words spoken. How can we be surprised when, as a muscle group, this skill set has been under assault like never before? We are always plugged in, online, connected, super available, super responsive, always on, always busy, always doing stuff, oh and by the way – juggling all of the eye-watering information with which our senses are being assaulted, (and to which I alluded in the very first chapter of this book). Jim Canterucci[16,] believes that powerful leaders are active leaders. His premise is that the most influential leaders are powerful listeners. Isn't it true that it's too easy to listen in order to speak, rather than to listen to *really understand?* Canterucci[16] espouses that there is a big difference between hearing and listening and quotes research that would suggest that most people forget 50% of what they hear within moments of hearing it. Again, how startling is that?

Listening Louder

Leadership can all too easily be viewed in terms of 'tell'. The best leaders with the most engaging presence listen louder. What do I mean by that? Quite simply literature categorizes how we listen in a wide variety of different ways. It can be described as combative, attentive and reflective or deep and light listening or fake and real etc. etc. You get the idea. In terms of best practice, much like many things in leadership, the theory is not intellectually challenging, it's the practical application of it that is the tough part. My narrative structure for demonstrating presence as a leader through listening is as follows:

Level 1 - Cosmetic Listening (In Other Words, I'm Not Listening)

Cosmetic Listening is 'pretending to listen'. Just

because someone is making a noise in your direction, it doesn't mean that you're listening. Effectively, when we're listening cosmetically what that means is that we're 'in our own head' thinking about something else, focused on something else, absorbed by something else – but we are most certainly not listening to the other person who is making a noise in our direction. How effective we are at 'faking it' will determine whether or not others realize what's going on. For example, we may be looking right at someone, we may be nodding our head and making verbal cueing noises ("I see", "hmm" etc.). Occasionally with this sort of listening we will get caught out if the person asks us a question, and we will have to ask them to repeat it.

Despite the fact that in reality we all do cosmetic listening from time to time, isn't it funny that when the behaviours are written down in front of our eyes it just looks like we are, on occasion, incredibly rude? What I've noticed in business today is how much of the cultural norm in business now is *not to listen.* We are so wedded to our technology that it seems to be perfectly acceptable to multi-task, whilst allegedly communicating with each other at work.

So, let me be clear. If you want to convey presence as a leader – put your device down and pay attention. No matter how much the norm of your organization is to pick up and put down your technology every three nanoseconds, don't succumb to it. If you want to *engage* people; *motivate* people; *appreciate* people;

ignite people but simultaneously you are demonstrating *that you can't be bothered to listen to people,* then let's just be clear, you're not conveying presence. It's about the biggest compliment you can pay someone and it's a lot harder than it might appear.

Level 2 – Conversational Listening (Sorry, I Am Still Not Listening)

Conversational Listening is what we do most of the time. Stephen R. Covey in his global best seller[17] suggests that "most people do not listen with the intent to understand; they listen with the intent to reply". This is conversational level listening at its best (or worst). Our focus when we operate in this way is to enter the conversation. We have something to say; we're waiting for you to stop talking; or take a breath; or to pause; or for God's sake we're waiting for you to just shut up. When you don't and when we can't contain ourselves any further we just start talking over you. That's when we know we're listening conversationally. We cannot multi-task by talking and listening at the same time so sorry; we are still not listening.

Level 3 – Active Listening (Hurrah, I Am Listening – A Bit)

Active Listening does what it says on the tin. For the first time so far, we are demonstrating that we are listening by paying attention to the person speaking. We are making more effort to focus on listening than to focus on speaking. The thing about active listening is that we're listening with more than one of our senses. We are listening both with our verbal and non-verbal body language in order to convey that we hear what the person is saying. This means that we might use verbal nods (as we do at the cosmetic listening level) but this time we're paying attention, plus we might ask questions, we might use repetition and we might summarize what we've heard. At the level of active listening we hear both content and start to discern context.

Level 4 – Exquisite Listening (Wow, I Am Right in the Zone)

Let's be clear. To listen exquisitely is utterly absorbing, engaging and exhausting. We know we've been listening more deeply when we're tired! At this level our mind is quiet and still, and our focus is completely on the other person. Not only are we listening to them with our senses, but we're also listening at an even deeper level such that we have a deep connection of rapport in that moment. At the level of exquisite listening not only are we able to hear what's being said and what that means, but we are also able to hear what's *not being said,* and what is really meant. Peter Drucker[18], one of the world's most brilliant thinkers on leadership and development said: "the most important thing in communication is to hear what isn't being said". As always, Drucker was right.

The Importance of Non-Verbal Communication

How much talking do you think you do in a day? Let's say it's a busy day with calls, meetings and so on. It will be less than you think. If we add up the number of moments when words come out of our mouths, times that and then add them all together, we will be going some to be talking for more than between three to four hours in a day. Often people will look at me askance when I say that, but it's true. We talk for less time than we think we do. Now, the exceptions for those of you desperate to disprove this fact are, of course, if you're delivering three lots of a two-hour presentation with a few questions at the end. Yes, if that's you, then you're talking for a lot longer than three to four hours. However, come on, how many of you reading this would typify that as a normal day? For the rest of us the point is simple. We talk for a lot less time than we think we do.

We learn an eye-watering number of postures, gestures and signals from birth through to the age of five and as primates, we pay attention to what others around us are doing, infer meaning and copy it. This whole facet of our communication toolkit is well honed and we need, as leaders to understand what has become habitual about our body language that is positive (so do more please), and, what has become unhelpful, contradictory or even destructive (so we need to stop it).

A simply brilliant TED talk is that given by Amy Cuddy[92]. Cuddy is an Associate Professor at Harvard Business School and her personal story is a fantastically inspirational one all of its own and worth watching for that reason. As a social psychologist she shows that how we arrange our own body, or how we 'pose', impacts our levels of testosterone and cortisol in the brain and as a result, impact our feelings of confidence. In other words, adopting a posture of confidence can improve our feelings of confidence. The point is this. We are a system and our brain, emotions, body are all connected. As a consequence, we can impact one by changing another. As leaders if we want to convey presence then we ignore this whole area at our peril.

Misquoting Mehrabian

And while we're at it, talking about body language and the importance of it, let me just take you on a tiny detour. In my first book 'Brandtastic or Brand Terrible'[80] I talked about the extent to which statistics on non-verbal communication are widely misquoted. Alfred Mehrabian conducted some research[81] in the 1970s that explored the notion of how communication was impacted by expressions, gestures and vocal tone that aligned or contradicted with the spoken message. He designed several experiments that revealed that 7% of the communication of emotion was derived from language, 38% was derived from vocal tone and 55% from the visual message. This research has been widely and extensively misquoted to suggest that in all communication 7% happens in the spoken word, 38% through voice tone and 55% via body language. This is simply not true.

With all of that said and to be reiterate; persuasive, positive, compelling body language remains a critical component to conveying presence and all leaders need to be honest about where their strengths and gaps lie.

De-coding Body Language

The thing about body language is that as soon as we talk about it; we then think we're able to interpret everything that others are communicating non-verbally. It's as if we think we're suddenly in a groovy club. So, here's a word of warning. An anthropologist said to me that part of the reason why body language as a topic within the corporate world has suffered as a brand is because it was poorly understood and badly applied. He offered three golden rules and I feel the need to repeat them before I talk about each area that is critical to the notion of presence and funnily enough, it's a group of three things:

1. **Clusters:** Never try and interpret a single gesture in isolation. Just because someone might be scratching their nose, it does not mean that they are lying. It may just mean that they have to scratch their nose. It's like trying to understand a word without the rest of the sentence.

2. **Congruence:** Research shows that non-verbal signals carry about five times as much impact as verbal communication and when the two are incongruent, many individuals (especially women), rely on the non-verbal message about the verbal content. What does that mean? Essentially what it means is that when conveying Executive Presence there needs to be congruence (and not conflict) between what we're saying and what we're doing whilst we are saying it.

3. **Context:** In other words, what is the environment in which the body language occurs? If you are sat in a senior leadership meeting and are being extensively scrutinized for a project proposal for example, being sat there with arms crossed and legs crossed might mean that you feel extremely uncomfortable and feel defensive. If, however, the room is freezing cold then it might just mean that – that you are cold.

Making our Non Verbal Communication Work For and Not Against Us
Handshake Heaven or Hell?

Now, this is a topic about which I could write a book all on its own. How often will we shake hands over the course of our career? My guess is hundreds of thousands of times – at the very least. And yet, despite this, how many times have we had clear, proper training on this. Everything I am about to lay out is set against a western, business culture and I make this point because I am incredibly aware of cultural considerations and norms. Any professional who travels internationally has to make time to understand some of the cultural differences and considerations regarding the greeting gesture.

The history of handshakes began as far back as the days of the Roman Empire. During those times, men used to grasp each other's lower arm (or wrists), as a common way of greeting each other. The original intent of such a gesture was to ensure that a dagger was not concealed up the sleeve. However, by the turn of the 19th century, the shaking of palms became the most common gesture to cement a commercial deal or agreement between two parties.

It appears extraordinary to me that we rarely (if ever), have proper training on the etiquette of shaking hands properly. And yet, we will form immediate, sometimes very emotive, impressions and reactions to those we meet if we experience a handshake that we do not like. We also almost *never* comment on what we've just experienced either. Remember, the purpose of a handshake is to signal the beginning of a warm, friendly encounter.

We also continue to witness unending examples of politicians, world and business leaders who persist in getting it wrong.[83, 84, 85, 86, 87, 88, 89, 90, 91]. I have referenced a number of pictures in the bibliography that are absolutely fascinating and well worth a look. Every rule in the book is broken when it comes to handshakes, and the fact that it is continually picked up by commentators and written about at length merely serves to reinforce the importance and significance of getting this gesture right, not wrong.

Handshakes to Avoid if You Want to Convey Presence

The Vice: I have come across this handshake far too many times in my career. It appears to be a favourite of men who want to dominate and assume early control of the relationship. Their palm is presented flat and downwards, as opposed to being presented sideways; there is a short, sharp pump of the hand and the grip. My goodness, it's a grip that can stem blood flow.

The Wet Fish: This is where the palm which is presented cold, clammy and lacking any firmness. It is widely associated with communicating a weak character and can create the impression of being very ineffectual. Another take on the gesture is that it can be perceived as a lack of commitment to the encounter. Earlier I mentioned the notion of cultural considerations and certain cultures do shake hands more softly because a firm handshake is considered offensive. Examples might include Asians and Africans. As always, the cultural context must be taken into consideration. One of my clients suffered from a condition called hyperhidrosis, which is a genetic condition that causes chronic sweating. His (unrealized) habit was to wipe his hand on the back of the legs before shaking another person's hand. Unfortunately, of course, those who were about to do so tended to witness this gesture and considered it most off putting. Naturally! We strategized around it with things such as carrying tissues in the pocket so that he was able to put his hand in his pocket to remove the moisture before shaking hands. This solution was much nicer all round.

The Finger Tip Tussle: Again, I'm mindful of cultural considerations. However, this gesture can happen with encounters between men and women and it is where there is not full contact between the area of the thumb and index finger between the two parties, and so as a result, the fingers are grabbed. This gesture is actually demonstrative of wanting to maintain distance and can be seen as aloof. It's not an appropriate connection to make in western business and we need to make sure the curved area between the thumb and index finger of our right hand connects with the thumb and index finger when gripping the hand of our colleague.

The Bone Crusher: Oh dear God, I experienced this only last week with a client. It is where the hand is gripped and then the knuckles are sort of 'ground' by their hand in an absurdly aggressive and dominant way. I am, by dint of my profession, prompted to comment on it – which I did. I often wear on my right hand a piece of costume jewellery in the form of a dramatic ring, and it was honestly painful. Let's be clear. If our mind-set is to dominate then we can forget conveying presence. The rest of the world is not stupid. They can see exactly what is happening and we can forget trying to engage them. Let's stop this nonsense and get a different kind of a grip (literally and metaphorically).

The Stiff-Arm Thrust: One of the references in the bibliography, which I have listed above, provides lots of superb examples of this in action. Perhaps one of the most famous is the famous (or infamous depending on your point of view) photograph of the 'stiff-arm' thrust was taken at the White House. The year was 1993 and it involved the Israeli Prime Minister Yitzhak Rabin and the Palestine Liberation Organization Chairman Yasser Arafat. As President Bill Clinton looked on, it is one of the most perfect examples of this type of handshake and it is entirely designed to keep the other party at a distance and away from their personal space. Perhaps not surprisingly, given the history of the conflict between these two nations and the significance of the meeting and this gesture, we simply could not have expected anything more.

The Socket-Wrencher: Another absurd handshake. It is designed to set you off your feet and may be used by those who are trying to literally pull, drag you into their space. To do so, they have to almost yank your arm, so it's simply not a good experience. I am drawn to the phrase that we use in everyday language about 'getting off on the wrong foot'. I am not sure that this is connected with that but it's a perfect example of how our language can reflect what we do in terms of non-verbal communication. Another one to avoid.

The Pump Action: Look this is simply where we are just continually, endlessly shaking the other person's hand. The description comes from the fact that it may appear we are trying to pump water from a well. Two to three pumps is fine; a couple more if it's a particularly warm and friendly greeting, but please, know when to stop.

Making Your Handshake Count

The whole point of a handshake is that it signals the start of a warm, positive and friendly exchange between you and the person whose hand you are shaking. It's the basis of building rapport and hence two key ingredients are needed here.

- Firstly, it's important that both hands are in the vertical position so that no-one's hand is either (a) dominant or (b) submissive. I have literally at time of writing had to comment to a senior sales leader on his handshake towards me. It was palm down and trying to dominate. I believe he had no idea; but it's simply not acceptable and I commented to him on it. To his credit, he was embarrassed and asked for clarity and feedback on what he did and needed to change. The point is that the gesture elicited a visceral reaction in me. He needed to understand the consequences of his gesture. (And no doubt he gave me another hand gesture when I wasn't looking).

- Secondly, it's important to apply the same pressure as you receive. If you were meeting a number of people at once, you should expect to have to alter the intensity and angle of the handshake to create a feeling of rapport for each individual.
- Remember: men, you can, on average, exert twice the pressure of women because you shake harder, so be mindful and make allowances!! Handshakes should always happen at the same 'level'. So, if one person is sat down and someone comes over to shake hands, then stand up. Remember, the gesture is about parity. If two people are sat down and turn to shake hands then that is absolutely fine.
- The golden rule is simply this. Unless you and the other person have a personal or emotional bond, only use a single hand. Why? Because as some of the images in the bibliography beautifully show, this is supposed to be about parity, respect and equality. If it's a two-handed handshake where for one person has their hand covered by both of ours, then it conveys dominance.
- Who should reach out first? Confidence and presence comes from a willingness to initiate a handshake. However, we should always consider a couple of things before initiating the handshake. Am I welcome? Is this person happy to meet me or am I forcing them into it? What are the cultural considerations? (So, for example, in some cultures, for a man to reach out and shake a women's hand that would be considered inappropriate. Equally, for a woman to reach out and offer her hand to a

man, that would also be considered unacceptable –
in some cultures.)

- According to anthropologists, women who initiate
  a firm handshake first usually create a better first
  impression according to anthropologists than men.
  This is because this originates from what was
  exclusively a male gesture.

Eye Contact

The most intimate non-touching gesture is eye contact.
We convey a great deal through how we look (or not)
at others. Let's take some examples of expressions:
'she looked daggers at me' or 'he always looks down
his nose at me' or 'they've never seen eye to eye' and
so on. There are so many references to the importance
of eyes in our overall communication that it is right,
from the standpoint of conveying executive presence,
to start here.

Here's the thing. We *always notice* when others do not
give us regular eye contact and yet we rarely if ever
comment on it. Our conclusion when this happens is
not 'now there's someone who I can really believe and
trust in'.

I had a client who was invited to work with me
because he never looked his team members in the eye.
It caused significant challenges. How can we expect
our people to go into bat for us? To go the extra mile
for us when we can't even *look at them?*

There is some interesting research out of Holland[97] that tested the hypothesis of gaze and head tilt (more of that later), and its impact on our perception of others. Essentially what they found was that how we look at other people and the position of our heads as we do so can communicate responses that suggest we are perceived as friendly, hostile, receptive, antagonistic etc. The point is, this stuff all matters; much as we'd like to think it doesn't.

So, our first challenge is get the amount of time and regularity of looking at others right. I was taught by a hideous science teacher at school who always looked over the tops of all of our heads. He never actually looked at us. Being hideous teenagers ourselves, we realized the amount we could get away with in terms of pulling faces, sticking out tongues etc. because that's the way we were and obviously, immaturity was in full flow. The point was, we didn't respect him because he didn't build trust with us by looking at us and it defined our opinion of him.

Eye contact can also become a power struggle or a source of increased tension. Whenever we are having a row; we will look at the other person for longer and our eyes will widen. When we're under pressure, it's usually the first non-verbal signal to go, because we (at least initially) are trying to avoid confrontation. According to Allan & Barbara Pease in their book *The Definitive Guide To Body Language*[82] men tend to have a form of tunnel vision that makes them better equipped at seeing what is directly in front of them, whereas women have a much wider peripheral vision so they can be looking at another person's face, whilst simultaneously being able to take in a lot more information. Who cares I hear you ask? Well, here's the thing. Every time we see someone for the first time, even when it's someone we know well, we look at them from head to toe. It's a survival tactic. We need to know that the other person isn't going to be a threat.

Barbara and Allan Pease in their book *The Definitive Guide to Body Language*[82] reference a number of different types of ways that we look at people. Who knew?

The Social Gaze

Experiments into gazing reveal that during social encounters what we tend to do is look in a triangular way at the other person's face, moving between their eyes and mouth for the vast majority of the time. This is seen as most inclusive and non-threatening.

The Intimate Gaze

Look I think we just need to get over this because we all do it. When approaching from a distance, we will look quickly at the other person's face and then check out their nether regions. Look, the opportunity for humour here almost overwhelms me but I'll resist it.

We all do this; gentlemen because your peripheral vision isn't as good as women's (see later on where I talk about eye contact for the proof), you are extremely poor at getting away with this. So, be warned and beware is all I can say.

The Power Gaze

Well I find this one a bit odd I must say; but not uncommon and I have experienced it. It's where we look at the centre of the other person's forehead and then move between that area and their eyes. It's most peculiar to experience and it is, as the name suggests, a power play. Now, if our goal is to convey presence then this *isn't* the way to do it.

The Power Stare

Apparently there is one. The notion is where we are trying not to blink. If we also narrow our eyes as if to focus very intently on the other person, it can be very unnerving. My question is: why? If we are trying to engage, connect, inspire, persuade, galvanize others, why do this? I found this non-verbal strategy so peculiar that I tried it out with my cat at home and he didn't like it either.

The Extended Blinker

Anthropologists will tell you that this is an unconscious attempt by the person's brain to block you from their sight – for whatever reason. Rest assured that the reason is not a good one. Another client of mine (female this time) had this particular habit and her eyes were almost shut, and hovered shut for what was, relatively, a very long period of time. So, the experience was one of looking at someone who largely had her eyes shut. Even the words give it away. She was literally shutting the rest of the world out. It simply doesn't convey impact and presence.

So, what to do? 'Scanning' is the answer. 'Scanning' is simply the technique of regularly achieving momentary eyeball-to-eyeball contact with the audience, whether they are large or small (the audience that is; not the individual). If necessary, we'll need to move our body to be able to make that eye contact (often people do not). Any situation, be it a more formal presentation, a conversation at a table during a meeting with colleagues or when we find ourselves stood in a queue talking to three people whilst waiting for coffee. Look people in the eye.

Head Up

Who doesn't recall being told to lift their head up by parents when we slouched around as moody teenagers? Well, in adulthood we may or may not have built the right muscle memory in this area. Allan Pease[82] talks about three different types of position for our heads. The first is actually called the 'Head Up' position and it indicates neutrality in relation to what is being said. It remains quite still and doesn't move a great deal. If our head is lifted too high we are looking down (literally) on others, so not a good idea to build rapport and connection. The second is the 'Head Tilt' that does exactly what it says on the tin. If we look at advertising billboards or in printed or digital media, often the models have a tilted head and it's a submissive gesture where our throat is exposed and it's to make us appear less threatening. Look, if we need to convey confidence and authority, please don't do this. To show we're listening, convey empathy or understanding in a more pastoral context; then that's fair enough, but otherwise, it's to be avoided.

Can you guess what the third position for the head is? Not surprisingly perhaps, it's the 'Head Down'. This tends to suggest that we don't agree with what's being said or done. The phrase about just 'keeping your head down' would indicate that we're trying to avoid confrontation. The point is; it's another undesirable head position and utterly at odds with confidence and credibility.

To Nod or Not To Nod?

Well, we've all got to love a nodder. The point is, the speed of nodding indicates very different things. A slow nod is an encouraging signal of approval, understanding and listening. A fast nod suggests 'yes, I get it, move on'. I once worked for a manager whose favourite phrase was 'skip to the end'. Hideous I know, and nodding fast is non-verbally saying exactly the same.

Walk Tall

It may appear odd to read, but as an image professional, the first thing I pay attention to when working with a client is how they walk. Yes, how they walk. Our walk is a continual advertisement to the rest of the world about how we feel about ourselves at that particular moment. Our walk physically changes throughout the day if for no other reason than our spine compressing as we carry the weight of ourselves around. It relaxes back overnight when we sleep, but we can literally shrink by up to an inch during the course of a day. Leaders with presence 'walk tall'. Head up, chin parallel to the ground, straight back, a level gaze so that you can appreciate the view (as opposed to looking at the ground), not overloaded with kit and they stride confidently around the place. I was asked to work with a marketing leader who literally ran around the office. I had another client who was a successful sales professional but, wherever she went she almost ran to client meetings. Whenever her boss or other senior leaders came out to work with her for the day and to see her clients, they noticed how frantic and hectic her pace was. The point is, whilst she was very successful and her clients clearly loved her, there was a brand conflict because of what she was communicating by beetling around all over the place. There is nothing about her behavior that conveyed presence. Instead what it was saying was panic, chaos, tension and a lack of organization.

Our Hands Reveal Our Inner Thoughts

Jo Navarro wrote an international best-selling book called '*What Every Body Is Saying*'[93]. Navarro has been studying non-verbal behavior for the past 45 years and 25 of those were spent at the FBI, catching spies. In many ways, our hands are quite simply extraordinary because of their ability to enable us to do the most amazing things – play cricket (bet you didn't think I was going to say that), play an instrument, paint, write, build, create and so on. Navarro's point is quite simple; that being there is almost nothing our hands do that is not directed by our brain. Whether that is conscious or unconscious. In other words our hands reveal what our brain is thinking and they are extremely effective in helping us to convey presence if used effectively. So, how do we do that?

Make them Visible

Hands on show help to build trust as opposed to hands that are hidden. Hidden hands convey a negative impression. Think about when you stand up to present in front of a large group. Whether that is a skill that you are well versed in or not, one of the most challenging things to learn how to master was your hands.

Use them for Emphasis not Exaggeration

If you asked an Italian friend of mine what would happen if you tied their hands behind their back, they would reply that they would be unable to speak. Using our hands to reinforce and emphasize critical messages represent high confidence gesturing and is both persuasive and impactful. Using them all the time is not. It can be both distracting and irritating.

Learn to Steeple

Hand steepling is one of the most high confidence hand gestures and it involves slightly spreading our hands and then bringing them together to touch at the tops of the fingers. The name naturally comes from what appears to be the creation of a church steeple. The suggestion behind such a gesture is that we are confident in what we are saying.

Thumbs Up and Out

Thumbs up are an almost universal sign of confidence and, interestingly, status. Navarro[93] references John F. Kennedy as a former US President who was regularly photographed with his hands in his pockets but his thumbs on show. Having your hands in your pockets but your thumbs out is perceived as high confidence, however, if you put your thumbs in your pockets and leave the rest of your hands out the opposite is true.

Batoning

An example of using the hands positively for emphasis is the recent (at time of writing) UK election when all the candidates from the main parties used the 'batoning'[94] gesture. Essentially this is where the hands are placed vertically and used when we need to stress a key message. Creating some space between our hands is expansive and shows confidence as we look to take up space to reinforce key messages.

Deliberate, Measured, Movements for Emphasis

The use of our hands to reinforce what we say is most emphatic when we make deliberate, measured movements with some rigidity in our hands. Think about it. When we go to sleep at night our hands are gently curled to indicate being relaxed. So, when we want to bring authority and conviction to our messages it makes sense to straighten our hands and make them more rigid.

Avoid Certain Gestures that can Offend

One such gesture is pointing. Across the globe pointing our finger can be viewed as highly offensive. David Cameron, the UK Prime Minister, has clearly been coached on keeping his index finger under control so that when he makes a point, his hand is clenched so that it is not quite a fist, and the thumb is placed with the other fingers. The point is that he has to avoid replacing one aggressive hand gesture with another and this is distinctly softer and more impactful than pointing or clenching a fist.[131]

Preening

Preening ourselves in anyway (for example pulling at thread, removing fluff or lint – whether it's there or not), is not a high confidence gesture. Think about it. Effectively it's saying that we're more absorbed in ourselves than in you. Biting nails is never good either because what do we associate it with? Nerves.

Fiddling and Twiddling

With our hair, fingers, pens, papers (Gordon Brown, ex UK Prime Minister was renowned for continually shuffling papers[96]), our phone, laptop or any other fascinating piece of technology is simply a distraction and conveys a lack of confidence, nerves, boredom, disdain and/or contempt.

Hand Wringing

As a phrase that has come into our language, we already know what this means. We are concerned, angst ridden and/or indecisive. Nothing good going on here so let's not do that.

The Jingle Jangle

I've made this name up for one of the most infuriating ticks that I see, almost exclusively in men. What is that I hear you ask? Well, if you've not already guessed it's that infuriating leg tapping or knee bouncing movement that just goes on and on and on. Everything about this suggests a nervous energy that is dissipated by bouncing our leg or knee continuously. Leaders with presence have poise, and that means not looking like they either need the loo or are having a muscle spasm. Again, please stop.

Taking Up Space

Who is your favourite superhero? Mine is Diana Prince, otherwise known as Wonder Woman[99]. You may have chosen Batman[100], The Incredible Hulk[101] or someone else. The point is that there is some consistent and very deliberate body language that is associated with the messages that we get from them. Strength, confidence, power is all convey in their posture. Quite simply they take up space. I read a fantastic article in Time Magazine[102] that asked the question: 'Are You A Spreader?' The article references a study from a visiting professor at Massachusetts Institute of Technology and a fantastically named study called 'The Ergonomics of Dishonesty: The Effect of Incidental Posture on Stealing, Cheating and Traffic Violations'[103]. Their premise was to explore whether posture impacted the decisions we make and it relates to the work of Amy

Cuddy, whom I mentioned earlier. The bottom line is that how we position our body impacts levels of testosterone and cortisol in our body and hence how we feel. The study found that cars with more expansive seats were more likely to be guilty of parking illegally in New York. Two conclusions: environments where we are encouraged to expand our body can lead to people feeling more powerful (terrific), and secondly that these feelings of power can cause dishonest behavior (less terrific).

So, what does this mean, assuming we don't live in New York and drive a car there? In terms of 'Executive Presence', if we 'go small' we demean, reduce and make ourselves less significant, less successful, less relevant. So who wants that? Absolutely no one. In my experience, women can be more guilty of what I term 'tidying themselves' away in a meeting so as to take up less space, whereas men are more naturally comfortable to take up the space they need. That is not meant to be a sideswipe at our male colleagues, far from it. The reality is simply that this is what men tend to do naturally. An amusing but true story to reinforce that comment was a brilliant story I read before Christmas 2014 on this exact topic. In New York City (a place with which I have had a life-long love affair, by the way), the issue of 'manspreading'[104] was such that this posture was actually banned on public transport. I think this is a highly progressive and innovative policy as someone who battles on the train in the morning with commuters who (if male) tend to spread themselves across multiple seats and are blissfully unaware of the space and impact that they are having on their fellow commuters.

Our Body Talks

It's doing the vast majority of our communication as leaders and conveying our Executive Presence. There's a lot to think about and I invite you to reflect and pick and choose those non-verbal behaviours that you either need to do more of or do less of. Also never forget the informal moments – whether it's the canteen, the queue for coffee, travelling on public transport together, meeting at an event etc. These are all moments to demonstrate Executive Presence and in some ways, they are more meaningful because they are *unplanned*. One of my favourites is the 'corridor shuffle'. It's one of the occasions where we can see a colleague coming down the corridor in the opposite direction and our challenge is to know whether or not to make eye contact with them. Worse still, we're thinking 'I know that person but can't remember their name'. The point is, whether you are strolling into the office, moving from meeting to meeting or just 'hanging out'; you're communicating your presence, confidence and charisma. Make sure your body is talking the right message and one that you want the rest of the world to see.

Chapter Seven –
Deliberate Like A Leader

*"Truly successful decision-making relies on a balance
between deliberate and instinctive thinking"*

Malcolm Gladwell

What is meant by Deliberate?

Our friends at the Oxford English Dictionary[3] describe
the meaning of deliberate as 'done consciously and
intentionally; careful and unhurried; fully considered
and not impulsive'. Synonyms for 'deliberate' include
intentional, calculated, conscious and studied. You get
the picture. Interestingly, when I started this project I
didn't actually think that a facet of Executive Presence
that I would talk about is what actually goes on in
what the NBC TV show 'The West Wing' called 'one
square foot of real estate'. Of course on reflection it is
absolutely essential to consider how we deliberate as
leaders because, of course, this *determines how we
communicate.* Specifically what my research
determined was that leaders who have Executive
Presence and who 'engage' others are quite simply
able to do this:

How you think; your preferences for processing information; how you make decisions, solve problems, manage complexity, prioritize, strategize and rationalize business issues.

What We Asked

Reminding you that one of the questions posed from the survey was:

The Decisions Which Demonstrate Executive Presence

This section aims to understand your views on how Leaders made effective decisions.

The narrative structure for answering the following questions was as follows:

- *Strongly agree*
- *Agree*
- *Neither agree nor disagree*
- *Slightly disagree*
- *Strongly disagree*

In crisis situations, people with Executive Presence make decisions that are:

- *Well considered*
- *Based on extensive research*
- *Made quickly*
- *Based on consultation*
- *Consistently applied*
- *Communicated clearly*
- *Based on facts*
- *Based on intuition*
- *Based on a combination of facts and intuition*

In times of uncertainty, people with Executive Presence make decisions that are:

- *Well considered*
- *Based on extensive research*
- *Made quickly*
- *Based on consultation*
- *Consistently applied*
- *Communicated clearly*
- *Based on facts*
- *Based on intuition*
- *Based on a combination of facts and intuition*

In making important decisions about their company's future, people with Executive Presence make decisions that are:

- *Well considered*

- *Based on extensive research*
- *Made quickly*
- *Based on consultation*
- *Consistently applied*
- *Communicated clearly*
- *Based on facts*
- *Based on intuition*
- *Based on a combination of facts and intuition*

In making decisions that affect others' lives, people with Executive Presence make decisions that are:

- *Well considered*
- *Based on extensive research*
- *Made quickly*
- *Based on consultation*
- *Consistently applied*
- *Communicated clearly*
- *Based on facts*
- *Based on intuition*
- *Based on a combination of facts and intuition*

So, we deliberately asked how respondents make decisions in different contexts.

What the Research Revealed

In crisis situations, respondents prioritized the following three criteria to effective decision-making:

- Based on a combination of intuition and fact
- Well considered
- Consistently applied

What struck me about this what that one might assume in a crisis situation that making decisions quickly would be the most important. 11.0% of respondents actually disagreed or strongly disagreed that crisis decisions should be made quickly. Overall however, whilst speed was important, it was not seen as important as these three criteria.

In times of uncertainty, respondents expect leaders with Executive Presence will increase their levels of research and consult widely with others. In other words, whilst using fact and intuition and being well considered were still seen as important, what was distinctly different when it comes to making decisions in times of uncertainty was the need and significance of doing more research and consulting more widely. In addition, the percentage of respondents who disagreed with decisions in times of uncertainty being made quickly trebled to 31.7%. So three times as many people *don't want leaders to make decisions quickly in times of uncertainty.*

When facing important decisions about the future of their company, it is expected that people with Executive Presence will make decisions that are well considered, based on consultation and based on extensive research. In other words, these three factors ricochet in terms of importance when it comes to making decisions in this *specific context.* In addition, the proportion of respondents who disagree with making decisions in this scenario continues to rise and stands at 53.7%.

When leaders with Executive Presence are making decisions that affect others' lives, there was little difference between the factors that were considered most important in this context and when decisions about the future of the company need to be made – with one key exception. Respondents either agreed or strongly agreed that decisions that affected people should be consistently applied, upholding a sense of fairness. 47.6% of respondents disagreed or strongly disagreed with these sorts of decisions being made quickly.

In summary, when describing how people with Executive Presence made decisions, respondents generally did not value decisions that were made quickly and they did not value decisions that were based on intuition alone. So, those of us who like to make quick and intuitive decisions need to have a care. Executive Presence, therefore, requires abilities to research, gather and interpret data meaningfully, balance the continual, conflicting pressure to make decisions quickly with ensuring that the right decision is made.

What About How We Think?

That's a perfectly reasonable question. Why talk about how we think, when this book is all about how we influence others through conveying 'Executive Presence'? Quite simply, because how we think determines how we make decisions. How we make decisions impacts how we communicate and what we convey to others. Therefore, how we think affects how others connect and engage with us. How we think impacts whether or not others will decide to follow us and support our recommendations or approach.

The Debate between Heart And Head

Have you ever completed one of those psychometric, behavioural or communication styles assessments? Are you extrovert or introvert? Do you have red energy or green energy? Are you 'ask assertive' or 'tell assertive'? And on and on they go. Often, as part of the assessment you receive feedback regarding how you make decisions and it reveals whether or not you tend to make decisions based on your heart (instinct) versus your head (facts, figures, numbers). Every single assessment I've ever completed has put me at the 'head' end of the spectrum. I need objective data, information, facts and figures before I'll make a decision. I like to rationalize my decisions. A very dear friend of mind always ends up being described in terms of the 'heart' side of the equation.

So, we're all either one or the other and that seems perfectly reasonable, doesn't it?

Fast Thinking and Slow Thinking

However, there is fascinating research and some brilliant books that would suggest something quite different. We're not as delineated in terms of our mental processing as we might like to think and that when making decisions, when forming judgments, when assimilating an opinion, there is a battle going on between our intuition and our logic. Professor Daniel Kahneman is a Nobel prize winning academic who is also a professor and Senior Scholar at Princeton University. His book, *Thinking, Fast and Slow*[132] is a New York Times best seller. Essentially Kahneman suggests that the way our mind works is based on the fact that there are two systems or processes at work.

System 2 is the part of our mind that we're aware of and it's great at solving problems. However, it requires more effort and acts more slowly. We need more time to arrive at the right answer. We have to complete more complex computations and this system requires what Kahneman describes as 'the subjective experience of agency, choice and concentration[132]'. A simple example of this would be to say if you're asked to solve a more complex problem whilst walking, the chances are that you will stop walking because this simple task takes up most of your attention.

By the way, if you're in any doubt, feel free to do the brilliant (and I use it all the time on training programmes) 'Invisible Gorilla Test'[133] which was devised by Chris Chabris from Union College, New York and Daniel Simons from the University of Illinois. It's amazing!

Let's get back to Kahneman's research. System 1 is fast acting, requires very little effort and occurs almost involuntarily. Examples he sites to illustrate the book include:

- Complete the phrase 'bread and ....'
- 2+2 = ?
- Read words on a large billboard
- Drive a car on an empty road
- Detect distance between objects

Kahneman calls this 'fast thinking'. He suggests that this way of mental processing is incredibly powerful but also totally hidden. It is the system that is actually most responsible for the things we think, believe, say and do. And here's how it works. What happens is that we don't even realize that our 'System 1' is in control and it is as if we are on autopilot for the majority of the entire time.

Who cares? I hear you ask this question and here's the point. System 1 takes over when System 2 would be more appropriate. In other words, our intuition can lead us to reach conclusions and make decisions when in actual fact our problem-solving (but much slower) mind should be at work. Here's one of many examples quoted from his work.

Meet Steve. Steve is mild mannered and good at detail. The question is simple – is he more likely to be a librarian or a farmer? Most respondents would answer that Steve is a librarian and they would be wrong. This answer is based on a bias or caricature of librarians. We do not have the facts at our disposal to answer this question and so we jump to conclusions. The facts would suggest given there are a great many more farmers than librarians, we will find more mild mannered, detail orientated men driving a combine harvester than saying 'quiet please'.

This simple example also reveals something else in relation to how we think – that being that it is an example of we all have - biases. Kahneman calls these 'heuristics'[132]. A layman might call this a 'rule of thumb' and we reach for these when in actual fact (and often without us even *realizing*), we are simply completely wrong.

The other area of Kahneman's work that fascinated me was the notion of 'priming'. Priming can affect our decision making again, in a way that we might not have realized. Lots of tests on this but again, a simple example quoted in his book is if we are exposed to the word 'food' and then asked to complete the following word SO*P. Most of us will complete the word 'soup' rather than 'soap' and this represents what is known as priming our minds to jump to a specific conclusion. Fascinating and devious isn't it?

So What?

Leaders who have Executive Presence have emotional intelligence. Emotional intelligence means being self-aware. *Any* information that enables us as leaders to be aware of ourselves, how we behave, what we think, how we are, can only be a good thing. When was the last time you sat and thought about how you think? Probably not for a while – if at all. And of course, how we think impacts all of our behavior and communication. Interestingly my research links to what Kahnerman is suggesting in terms of respondents wanting leaders to take more time when reaching decisions. Our people don't want us to make fast decisions in times of uncertainty; they want us to take more time to make the *right* decisions. So, how do we do that? Dear reader please read on.

How To Make Effective Decisions

Look, I realize that I have quoted a lot of resources in the book. I do so because there is simply a wealth of brilliant, insightful, clever academics, business leaders and entrepreneurs who can teach us so much about leadership. One of the most widely published (and I think simply brilliant) management thinkers and gurus is Peter Drucker[134]. I absolutely love his work and he is one of the most extensively published academics ever. A brilliant book of his is *The Effective Executive*[135] and in it Drucker devotes a whole chapter to decision-making. Executives make decisions and whether or not we are a senior leader; the principles of Drucker's research and approach hold sway. Essentially Drucker suggests that there are five elements to effective decision-making:

1. **Classify the Problem**: Is it a generic issue or challenge or is it exceptional? The point of this is to understand whether or not the decision can be reached by honoring a principle or whether it is truly exceptional.

2. **Define the Problem**: What are the outcomes that the decision has to accomplish? This is about understanding what the situation is all about and what is, and what is not in scope.

3. **Specify the Answer to the Problem**: essentially this is about deciding what's 'right'. Drucker talks about the notion of compromise here and the fact that there are only two kinds, which he illustrates with proverbs. The first is "half a loaf is better than no bread". The purpose of bread is to provide food and, therefore, half a loaf is still food. The other is "half a baby is worse than no baby at all". Drucker also suggests that there is little point worrying about what might happen because they rarely do.

4. **Turning the Decision into Action**: This is effectively about getting on with it and Drucker suggests that this is the most time consuming of the five steps.

5. **Feedback**: Quite simply, this is about the fact that people make decisions and so by definition, they have the capacity to be fallible. As a result, the ability to measure the effectiveness of the decision depends on facts and figures. Without this, we can't measure how good our decision was. Drucker didn't say this but one of my first bosses did; quite simply you can't manage what you don't measure and this applies to the quality of our decision-making as leaders, as well as a wide range of other tasks and activities that we undertake.

Drucker's approach is so thoughtful, measured, logical, rational, sound and appropriate. He has referenced many different corporate examples to provide the evidence to support his point. And yet it struck me that I couldn't possibly just reference him. There is far too much data that suggests (contrary to the research results), that sometimes we can't be measured and consistent in how we make decisions and for that, I have to turn my attention to the superb work of the authors of '*Freakonomics*'[139].

Thinking like a Freak[136]

It is ironic that I am talking about this book at this exact moment because as I write, it is the day of the FA Cup Final[137] in the United Kingdom. Why is that ironic? Because the book *Thinking Like A Freak*[136], written by Steven Levitt and Stephen J. Dubner starts with a football story. They describe a scenario whereby we, as the reader, are invited to imagine that we are one of the best football players on the planet. It is the World Cup final and the scenario is penalties. For those of you thinking 'I don't like football' (me neither), stick with this. Oh, by the way, football is soccer for our international audience. Now, let's get back to being the best footballer in the world. Our challenge is to decide where to place the ball. It's us against the goalkeeper and the stakes in professional terms couldn't be higher. Do we kick the ball to the left corner or do we aim for the right hand corner? Apparently 57% of penalty kicks are to the left, and 41% of penalty kicks are to the right. My maths makes that 98%, and here's where Dubner and Levitt pose a third option. What about shooting right in the middle of the goal? Apparently, only 17% of kicks are aimed at the middle of the goal – where effectively the goalkeeper is standing as you, (remember you're the one of the best players in the world), start your run up. Why is that? As they put it: "what if the goalkeeper *doesn't* dive? What if for some reason he stays at home and you kick the ball straight into his gut, and he saves it, without even having to budge? How pathetic you will seem!" The point of the story is simple. It is often the case that we may, as leaders, be faced with making decisions where the options seem obvious, however, on further, deeper reflection there's possibly another option. Our challenge as leaders is to work out how to find it.

Levitt and Dubner[136] offer some key strategies to problem solving and effective decision-making:

1. Be willing to say "I don't know". One of the things that I am continually struck by as an Executive Coach is how rarely this is said, and I have commented on it elsewhere in this book. However, in the context of 'deliberating' as one of the hallmarks of Executive Presence, being *unwilling* to say 'I don't know' impacts our ability to think effectively. This absolutely makes sense in relation to problem solving and strategizing, which is often what I help executives and teams to do. A specific recent example of this has been working with sales teams who are trying to find ways to move forward in relation to accounts and opportunities that they are managing. Sales professionals don't know what they don't know sometimes. In other words, they are not aware that there are things that they do not know and hence, draw inference, connection and conclusion where none actually exists. When working in such situations one of the rules that I have is that 'I don't know' should be one of the things that we say most often. Becoming aware that we don't know something is a powerful step forward

because it garners insight, increases creativity and encourages steps to action. If we don't get comfortable with the phrase 'I don't know' then everyone is wasting his or her time. It's not an interview or a court of law.

2. Ignore boundaries. This is a fascinating concept because it assumes there's a solution to what may seem utterly improbable or even impossible. A great example of this relates to the story of George Dantzig[138] who was a Stanford mathematician. During his first year at Berkley University in the United States, Dantzig arrived late for a maths lecture and saw on the blackboard two mathematical problems. He assumed that these were homework and so wrote them down to take away with him. It took him a while to complete the task and thought that the homework was a tad more challenging than usual. When he submitted that homework to the lecturer Dantzig was concerned that it wouldn't necessarily bode well for him because the lecturer merely asked him to leave it on a heap of papers in a messy office. It took six weeks for the lecturer to read what his brilliant student had done. The two tasks were not homework; they were world famous and hitherto unsolved problems in statistics. Dantzig had solved them and the moral of this true story is simple. The 'unsolvable math problem'[138] was no more. Assuming that we *can do it* and channeling mental energy on working out *how* is far more productive and effective than expending effort on ruminating whether or not it is possible.

3. Think like a child. That means think small. Take big, complex problems and break them down into much smaller pieces so that we can solve small parts of it. Dubner says: "you want to give from A to Z, and I just got us from A to B'[136]. Thinking like a child also means asking lots of questions. Those of you reading this who are parents know what small children do brilliantly is asking an unending stream of questions – some are silly, some are brilliant, but what children evidence is a relentless curiosity. As we get older and our opinions, bias, values and beliefs become formed, our ability to remain unbiased is challenged and we switch to knowing, or at least thinking we know, all the answers.

4. When faced with a tough decision, flip a coin. Dubner and Levitt[136] conducted an experiment that was effectively a digital coin toss. 60% of those who participated followed through on the decisions determined by the toss of the coin. Decisions that they were following through on including leaving a job and leaving a partner, so this is grown up stuff. The point the authors made was that for many participants of the experiment, once the decision was made, they had an emotional reaction to it (whether it was a very happy or a very sad reaction). "They knew before they came to us what they really wanted to do but just needed some help making the decision," says Dubner[136]. So, next time you are wondering what decision to make, there is some real validity in simply tossing a coin. This as an approach flies in the face of what the respondents to my research

wanted, (i.e. they wanted leaders to be measured), but sometimes that's just how it is.

5. Incentivize but don't manipulate. A lovely story in the book is that of *Smile Train*[140] which is an international charity that has what they call "a sustainable approach to a single, solvable problem: cleft lip and palate". The backstory is simply that, as perhaps we all know, charities spend a lot of time and effort – as well as money – trying to acquire new donors. A slight diversion but it does relate, there has been (certainly in the UK), a growing disquiet regarding the relentless nature of pursuing people once they start to donate. At time of writing this book, a heartbreakingly sad story appeared in the UK press[141] of a 92-year-old lady who sold poppies to raise money for service families and veterans who could not take the relentless pressure of being bombarded by charities asking for more money. She threw herself off Clifton suspension bridge. Just wrong at so many levels. However, it relates to the Smile Train story because the charity was very aware of dissuading potential donors from giving again if they were continually approached through fund raising appeals. So, Smile Train ran a "once and done' campaign that committed to donors that they would not be approached again if they provided a donation. Such an approach is fundamentally different to that received wisdom, but what it revealed was that people were twice as likely to donate and, on average, gave more money. Levitt and Dubner categorize this approach to problem solving as collaborative, and succeeded because it

was an honest, respectful approach to their challenge to raise more money, and it elicited an unexpectedly positive response.

Keeping It Very Practical

A very common challenge for leaders is carving out quality thinking time. The pace of business, the practical, 'back-to-back meeting' nature of scheduling that takes over the working day, business travel, working across time zones etc. etc. All these things mean that it can be incredibly challenging to make time to deliberate. So, let me wrap up this chapter by offering some of the very simple, practical ways to increase our effectiveness around thinking which some of my clients use very successfully:

1. Focus on your 'best time' of day and carve out time to think and deliberate during that portion of your day. Some of us are 'owls' and some of us are 'larks'. I like getting up early and getting on with it. However, I know that I become less creative, effective and productive by 8.30pm. Others of us may be less effective in the morning – and frankly might loathe early starts – but we really hit our stride later in the day and in the evening. Being aware of what works best for us is essential to drive high quality deliberation.
2. Reflect on some of the best decisions you made and identify *how* you did it. What did you do? What didn't you do? What information,

individuals, and insight did you use? My point here is that high performing individuals tend to focus on their performance when things go wrong. My view is that we should exercise *much more* curiosity when things go right.

3. Understand *how* you make decisions. What I mean by that is to be curious about what information you need to make a decision? Do you need the headlines and highlights or do you want all the detail? Is getting the decision made most important to you or is the process of arriving at the decision more important? It's not that there's a right and a wrong, it's just that knowing what your preferences are is always helpful. Not least to understand when you are struggling to reach a decision, (or getting frustrated because you're not getting what you need from others in order to do so), is always helpful.

4. Be aware of your own bias. It may be unconscious. We don't like to think of ourselves as biased but the reality is that we all are.

5. Get out of your normal working environment – literally. Where inspires you? Is it the park? The garden? The gym? A beautiful river? The coast? The countryside? My point is not that we disappear on a corporate 'away-day'; I'm simply saying that thinking powerfully when we're sat looking out of the same window every day doesn't really do it. I often work with clients while we're on the move – walking in a beautiful park in London for example. Connecting with nature can be inspiring, moving, energizing and the quality of the conversation is often extraordinary.

6. Beware the demon that is email. I read some superb research recently by Loughborough University[142] that reveals the cost of email interruption is greater than we might have originally thought. When we allow ourselves to be interrupted (by having our email on), we tend to (a) respond within 6 seconds (b) take on average 64 seconds to recover – in other words to get back into the mindset and return to what we were working on. That costs us in terms of productivity and performance. So – turn email off (along with the phone) when needing to do high quality thinking.

7. Beware of your physical and emotional needs. When you're tired, angry, bored, hungry, lonely, in need of doing some sort of physical exercise to get rid of any excess stress or frustration – then look out. Our capacity to be effective and high performing is dramatically impeded when physically and emotionally we are not in a great place.

8. Continue to develop your skills in this area. There is a vast array of superb training that can build critical reasoning skills, making decisions dynamically, problem reframing, strategic thinking skills amongst many others. In addition, if an external coach or mentor would help create the space for you to reflect, debate, consider as well as challenge and support you then – quite simply – make it happen.

9. Speed isn't as important as consistent and well balanced. Remember our research revealed that speed of decision-making was not valued by our

respondents – especially given the uncertainty in which we all continue to work. However, a well-considered and consistent decision-making approach definitely is appreciated.

10. The McKinsey research[54] *'Decoding Leadership'* revealed that one of the four most important traits of leadership in times of change, uncertainty and ambiguity is the ability of leaders to seek different perspectives. Leaders who are able to stay abreast of different organizations and how they are approaching similar commercial challenges, to keep on top of market shifts and the latest commercial data are better placed to make decisions on what is objective, unbiased information.

A Final Thought on Thinking like a Leader

I realize that there is a great deal more that can be said about thinking effectively, or 'deliberating' as my model calls it. In the context of Executive Presence, I want to go back to one of my early references, Dan Levitin's book *'The Organized Mind'*[36]. His book is so brilliant because he was curious about how we think. My point is that is simply genius. That's what we need to be about ourselves as leaders. At what kind of thinking are we superb? Where do we struggle? What pushes our buttons and gets us doing some of our best work and what doesn't? What gets in the way of making time to think? And what sorts of resources do we need, based on what has been laid out in this chapter, to develop our abilities in this area still further?

I'll sign off on this chapter and leave you to have a think about it.

Chapter Eight –
Evolve Like A Leader

"The two most important days in your life are the day you are born...and the day you find out why"

Mark Twain

What is Meant by 'Evolve'?

Our friends at the Oxford English Dictionary[3] would say that to evolve means "develop gradually" and synonyms include "progress, make progress, advance, move forward, make headway, mature, grow, open out, unfold, unroll, expand, enlarge, spread, extend". What we found 'evolve' to mean from the research and in the context of Executive Presence was: "How you maximize your potential, how you manage your career, your locus of control, finding and pursuing your passion, succeeding at your life's purpose."

Why 'Evolve'?

Here's a story for you. I read a piece in the Huffington Post[106] and subsequently watched the video. If you're having a bad day, or if you're feeling old, tired, cynical, bored, grumpy or jaded then this simply is the video for you. It involved an extraordinary woman who is still working. Her name is Florence Rigney and she is the oldest nurse still working in the United States. She works at Tacoma General Hospital in Washington. She is also 90 years old. And note the verb usage here. She *works* at the hospital. She's still working after 70 years. Although if you ask her, it's not work in the sense of slumping shoulders and sighing and saying 'oh, well, I've got to go to work". Florence Rigney has spent 70 years doing exactly what she wanted because all she ever wanted to do was nursing. What is so moving, inspiring and unique about this story – apart from the obvious – is that it's so rare.

A Dose of Reality

I was first moved to think about this notion of 'evolving' in the context of leadership based on a combination of personal experience and also what happened to three of my clients within the space of a mere three months. Let's start with my clients. The first example relates to the privilege that I had of working with a brilliant lawyer in Spain. Extremely bright, highly regarded, personable, kind, with a twinkle in his eye, this extraordinary man and I collaborated on a specific client engagement with which he wanted my support. Our sessions were done either face to face in Madrid or on the telephone. I remember speaking to him on a Friday morning from the car and he said: "Sarah, I am so excited about this opportunity and I really think we are really making progress". He was vibrant, upbeat, content, frantically busy. So far; so nothing unusual. On the Sunday evening after spending a weekend with his family he sat down. Perhaps he was planning to read, to relax, or to watch television. He never got out of the chair. A massive heart attack ended a brilliant family man in his personal and professional prime.

I then discovered that a troubled client of 28, with whom I had worked for over a year, died in the bath after suffering a fit. Then I lost a lovely man who I had known for eleven years from oesophageal cancer. He had been talking about heartburn for a while and in a previous life, I sold a blockbuster drug for reflux oesophagitis. David and I talked regularly about using this drug and I talked about watching more endoscopies than you could shake a stick at. Even so, David lost his battle for life from oesophageal cancer far too young. What's all this got to do with 'Executive Presence', other than as stories being incredibly sad? Fair question and so bear with me.

Top Five Regrets of the Dying

I am not remotely religious but I have read an article that really caused me to want to address the issue of death directly from a leadership perspective. It was first written in The Guardian and the article was called *'Top Five Regrets Of The Dying'*[107]. It was written based on the experience of a nurse who specialized in working in palliative care and spent the final moments with an extraordinary number of people. Bronnie Ware is an Australian nurse who specialised in caring for patients during the last 12 weeks of their lives. Her reflections were combined into a top five because there was such a recurring theme and the original went viral on social media after it was first published in 2012. One of the top five regrets that she heard from patients was 'I wished I hadn't worked so hard'. I totally appreciate the angle of regret in terms of missing family time, seeing your children grow up, missing the fun, intimacy as well as occasionally mundane nature of family life. The phrase from her commentary that particularly struck me was 'all of the men I nursed deeply regretted spending so much of their lives on the treadmill of a work existence'[107].

Okay, here's my point. Beyond the obvious of 'life's too short', if there's one thing that working with my clients has taught me again and again it's that when people are doing things that they love; that they enjoy doing, it's simply a fact that they tend to be disproportionately good at it. When we are 'on our purpose' as a phrase I use, or pursuing our passion, then we are not only excelling, but also we love it at the same time. Spending time with, and working for, people who are 'on their purpose', that's inspiring; that's engaging; that's attractive as a leader. We want to be around people who are enthusiastic, passionate, and positive and we're quite prepared to work harder, give more and go the extra mile for those people. Contrast that with those who are fed up, depressed, resentful, tired and jaded. There's nothing about that which inspires or engages others.

My Story

I didn't know what I wanted to be when I grew up. I had a brother that always wanted to be a policeman (and he was, rising to the level of Inspector in the Metropolitan Police in London). I also had a sister who loved sport – especially football – and enjoyed a very successful career at Sky Sports and latterly the BBC, commenting on a wide range of sports, including her first love, 'the beautiful game'. They always knew what they wanted to be, pursued it and succeeded. As I approached my teens, that lack of clarity regarding my own professional future remained but I worked hard – very hard – at school and managed to secure a place at Nottingham Trent University. What was my degree of choice? Business Studies, which I picked because my reasoning was that it was sufficiently broad to be relevant to a wide range of potential roles. I was still keeping my options open as you can probably tell.

Four years later, after falling in and out of love, having many laughs, doing a lot of travel, holding down three jobs simultaneously to fund my degree and still having a load of debt, plus doing a good old-fashioned dose of growing up, I left university – but still none the wiser as to what my career would be. I worked in the US for six months doing a summer job to fund travelling and then came back to London. I didn't attend any of the university 'milk round' interviews during my last year at Trent because I thought I was going to Australia to travel after I'd been to the USA. The concept of 'gap years', which are now the norm, were not common during my time (1980s), but it turns out I couldn't afford it so came back to London to look for work. I was broke and still none the wiser as to what I wanted to do, so I got what was effectively an administrative role at a training organization. The best part of that job was that I met two of the most important women in my life who are simply exquisite and very dear friends of mine to this day. If there was one subject I *hated* at school, it was science. I mention that now because in my drive to clear my student debt, I left the London job and joined Astra Pharmaceuticals selling ethical medicine to doctors. Good grief! Yes I had a car, a bonus and a lot of fun but it was science!!!!!!! I hated the science aspect of it and that was compounded by the regulatory necessity of sitting a hideous exam within two years in order to remain being allowed to sell ethical medicines.

Ten years later I left, joined a very small training business and it wasn't until I hit my mid-thirties that I started to realise what would make my eyes dance. Helping others access more of their professional potential was what I loved doing, plus I wanted to start my own business. As a landmark birthday approached, that's precisely what I did, and combined it with training in professional image. Clothes and fashion have always been a passion of mine, but my focus, as always, has been on professional men and women. Now, ten years on and in my late forties, I can honestly say that I am 'on my purpose', although it's taken me a while to get here.

Why You Will Fail to Have a Great Career[143]

One of the best, best, best TED talks I have watched in the last twelve months is by Larry Smith, a Professor of Economics, University of Waterloo in Canada. It's a funny, but very blunt, talk that will make you stop and think – if you've not already done so given the title above. His unique delivery style is thought provoking, funny, and devastatingly honest and it's a video that we all should watch and re-watch. Smith states that most of us will fail to have a great career and espouses the reasons why:

1. Some of us start out with the aspiration for a good career and some of us start out with the aspiration for a great career. However, most of us will fail at both.
2. We have been told many, many times that we should pursue our passion, but choose to ignore this advice and decide not to pursue it.
3. Some of us are simply too lazy and won't try hard enough. If we try to look for our passion, but not find it, then we make excuses not to do what you need to do for a really great career.

4. We create excuses that we believe, such as the excuse that really great careers are truly a matter of luck for most people.

5. We choose to believe that there are special people who pursue their passions but they are geniuses. Smith suggests that we all used to think we were geniuses – but probably only when we were young. As we grow up we lose this belief and think instead that we are 'completely competent'. Smith believes that such thoughts damn us all with the faintest of praise. And he's right.

6. We believe that if we pursue a great career then we have to be weird. People who pursue their passions are strange or odd. We don't like to think of ourselves as strange or odd. We like to think of ourselves as nice, normal people. However, nice normal people don't have passion.

7. We do what our parents tell us – and that is to work really, really hard. Smith believes that we can work really, really hard – and that's not the same as having a really great career. He also believes that just telling kids to work really hard is nonsense. Why? Because all of the evidence points to the contrary.

8. We find things that we're interested in but we don't find our passion. Smith says that having an interest is great – but what about finding our passion in the big wide world and trying a bit harder? We're not interested. Passion isn't the same as interest and we might have lots of interests but all of us need to find our *passion*.

9. Even if we find our passion many of us will still fail according to Smith. Why? Because we

continue to invent excuses for not having a *great* career as our passion. The phrase *"if only I had..."* is, according to Smith, one of the most damning things we can say.

10. Smith says that what we say to ourselves is that human relationships are more important than accomplishments. We want to be a great friend, a great parent, a great spouse etc. and we won't sacrifice that at the altar of human accomplishment. Smith is uncomfortably honest here. If we listen to what we're saying to ourselves; we're making ourselves out to be a hero. But we're no heroes.

11. Then when our children say that they want to be something other than that which they are good at, we repeat the mantra. We repeat what our parents told us and what we have told ourselves in terms of excuses.

12. The bottom line is that many of us are simply afraid. We're afraid to try, afraid to fail, afraid to succeed.

13. Unless..........

It's Time for a Change?

The Harvard Business Review published a great short article on '5 Signs It's Time For A New Job'[108]. Essentially there is psychological research which supports the thinking that there are five key signs that it's time for a change of career. The five signs below are credited to this article[108]:

1. **You are not learning**: the notion being that happiness comes from lifelong learning. This connects to the personality qualities of creativity and curiosity.
2. **You are underperforming**: if we are operating on 'cruise control', where we could almost do our role whilst asleep, then it's another sign for a change. We want to operate in a way where we can perform to our best.
3. **You feel undervalued**: and here we come back to the notion of 'engagement'. People want and need to feel appreciated and when they don't, they are far more likely to experience stress and burnout, as well as impacting the engagement of those around them. Worst-case scenario here is descending into criminal behaviour such as theft and vandalism.
4. **You are just doing it for the money**: of course, it's not uncommon for people to stick with a job just for the money; but in the long term it's soul sapping. It's hard to be inspiring, engaging, motivational, inspirational for others when what we're doing isn't attracting our best self at work.
5. **You hate your boss**: people join companies but leave managers. That's just a fact. Harvard Business Review article[108] comments that employee engagement is three times more dependent on what they term 'intrinsic' versus 'extrinsic' rewards. In other words, we value enjoyment, sheer curiosity, learning or personal challenge far more than financial rewards.

The Locus of Control

What used to be the world's best-selling business book (it is no longer – but it's still brilliant), was written by Stephen Covey. *'Seven Habits Of Highly Successful People'* reveals, well, exactly what you'd expect given the title. One of the 'habits' of highly successful people is the notion of the locus of control. Effectively, this is all about mindset. We know the expression (I'll clean up the language) about there being three kinds of people in the world. Those who make it happen, those who watch it happen and those who wonder what on earth happened. The locus of control suggests that those who make it happen have a high 'internal' locus of control. In other words, they rely on themselves to find a way forward, overcome an obstacle, resolve an issue and make things work. Those individuals with a high 'external' locus of the world are focused on the rest of the world doing what it needs to in order for them as individuals to be happy, have what they want, get on, get ahead and so on. We have to focus on what we can do and let go of that which we can't.

Finding (and Staying True to) Your Purpose

It's unlikely to appear in a moment of inspiration whilst you're peeling potatoes. So, we need to know how to get started on this. I offer below a mixture of practical and more soulful strategies. All of them work. Pick and choose.

1. **Evolve your own Personal Brand**. Everyone has a personal brand whether they realize it or not. People like me spend much time with professionals helping them to define their personal brand because most professionals are 'branded' accidentally. By that I mean we fail to capitalize on our strengths, whilst continuing to be sabotaged by our perceived weaknesses. Our brand should be distinctive, relevant and obvious. It should also represent the *essence* of us as unique individuals. We are always communicating our brand and hence our job is to ensure that it aligns with, rather than contradicts the brand perception *that we actually want.*

2. **Make quality time to think about what you really want.** What I find so extraordinary is how often I hear the 'I'm too busy' mantra. Show me your bank statement and your diary and I'll tell you what you care about. In other words, it's always a choice. Our time is totally ours to give away and we make choices every day about how we do so. If we're too busy for this, then what's more important than thinking about how we want to spend our time providing for others and ourselves in a way that makes us not also responsible *but also happy*? Our happiness is our responsibility. I don't mean by the way that we can make time to think about it for five minutes between conference calls. I mean make time and take time to step away, think, breathe, be creative, daydream, and fantasize about how we'd like to earn money and what we'd like to do next. My husband and I have what we call 'Brummitt

Summits' which happen at least twice a year, always whilst we're away on holiday and so away from work, chores etc. and can think and plan for the next year ahead – as well as reflecting on the year just past. It's not just financial stuff either; it's about our careers, our ups and downs, what we want more of and less of in our lives and we minute it and reflect on it later. Incredulity at this approach is tempered with the fact that we simply apply what we do in a work context to our lives together.

3. **Check in with yourself in terms of how often you spontaneously recognize how happy you are.** Because quite simply if you're not happy you're not giving your best self at work. It is *impossible* to be your best self (and enable others to be as inspired, engaged, motivated and moved by you), as they could be if you aren't happy. And can we just pause our cynical colleagues who are saying 'I have bills to pay and responsibilities to honour. I can't afford/don't have time to be just 'happy''. Why can't you have both? Or all three? Because my belief is that you can earn more and have more time if you get 'on your purpose'. Cue Larry Smith who I mentioned earlier. We *tell* ourselves we can't; and so we invested in proving ourselves right.

4. **Create a 'Circle Of Life'**[151]. No, this is not just a line from *The Lion King* and a cue to start singing. Draw a circle for each of the key 'chunks' of your life (e.g. health, career, family, money, fun – whatever you want them to be – it's your life) and ask yourself, *'how satisfied am I?'* Note, the

question is **not** '*how successful am I?*' The two things are not the same. I have worked with highly successful people who aren't happy and very happy people who aren't 'successful' in terms of money or status. The point about evolving is being satisfied. Are you? And where do you need to focus your efforts to be even more satisfied with your life (and work)?

5. **Stop Procrastinating.** If you can't find time to do this; then don't whine about it. You have the most to gain; your happiness, peace, joy, wealth and whatever else is important to you is at stake if you don't do this so know that it's always a choice when you choose not to.

6. **Write your own retirement speech.** A great tip. Imagine it's your very last day at work and someone is giving a speech on your working life and career. What would you want them to say? Now write it down. Don't feel shy, bashful or silly. Just do it. Now put it somewhere for continual reference. What you've written is what you really want. It's your purpose.

7. **Focus on what you can control.** And let go of that which you can't. Remember *Steven Covey's Seven Habits Of Highly Effective People*[53] book and *The Locus Of Control?* Even if something is incredibly frustrating and we have no influence over it (so a simple example might be the weather), then what we can control is our response to it. So, we always have choice.

8. **Surround yourself with people who are on their purpose.** This is motivating, inspiring and galvanizing. If they can do it; so can you. Spend

time with them learning how they did it. Stay close to them as well. They are one of your 'energizers' or 'radiators' (see the Resonate chapter to know what I mean by this. We all need some of those.

9. **Make where you are now part of your story.** A terrible temptation is to judge our self, criticize our self and focus on what we 'haven't done' or 'can't do now'. Beware. This can be extraordinarily debilitating and a recipe for inaction, depression and a sense of worthlessness. I spent several years being incredibly frustrated that I was not a FTSE 250 board executive. And then I realized that I had never planned to be. I had not pursued it. I had chosen a different path and my choice now was to work out what would make me happy with it. Doing so sets you free.

10. **Get to action.** As moving, motivating and magical as all this can read to be, if we don't do things then nothing will happen. However big or small, getting to action regularly turns what might feel a hopeless situation into a much more hopeful situation, step by step.

11. **Beware of your self-talk.** Larry Smith's brilliant TED talk[143] reminds us all of the need to pay attention to the lies we tell ourselves. Yes, the word 'lies' reads quite shockingly. However we do. We delude and deceive ourselves and let's not pretend otherwise. Someone said to me once 'show me a man's cheque book and calendar and I'll show you what he cares about'. And this is totally right. It's all within our gift to control – should we choose to.

12. **Get a career coach.** They can help with all the practicalities of what next and where next for you, as well as help strategize to get there. I have a client who is a senior leader in the digital market and he is someone with whom I have had the privilege of working with for more than ten years. I walk alongside him throughout his career – sometimes more closely (when we work together) and sometimes at a distance (when he does not need regular sessions). Ironically we spoke this morning – on the day of writing this chapter. The next stage of his journey has begun and it's very, very exciting.

13. **Go build links with other industries.** Finding out what others do is a great way to glean best practice to bring into the business. That gives you personal profile, helps the organization and energizes us. It also creates new possibilities and starts new conversations.

14. **Set yourself the challenge of being offered at least two jobs per year that you turn down.** Yes I know this sounds counter-intuitive but think about it. Most people look to move roles when they are unhappy. Far, far too late and totally the wrong dynamic when we feel we 'have' to do something. Saying 'no' doesn't lessen your chances of the job you want; it actually improves them.

15. **Get out of your comfort zone more often.** When we are out of our comfort zone as leaders then we really learn about ourselves. Always being comfortable, safe and in charge is a sure fire recipe for becoming less effective and more complacent.

It also erodes confidence. Our world gets smaller and our abilities diminish. Don't let that happen! Make a change, stick your hand up for a difficult project, take on board a 'problem person' – anything that isn't easy is usually a superb platform for learning, growth and development. It's up to us to grasp the nettle.

16. **Remember what you loved as a child.** People tend to be good at things they love and often what we loved as kids connects with our purpose. For me, I loved cutting out the clothes on the back of my Bunty[152] comic. I loved dressing up dolls. What I love as an adult is the image business. Who knew?

17. **Build your network intentionally.** It's all too easy to think that we don't like networking and that it represents a warm white wine and dodgy canapé in some ghastly hotel. It doesn't and it shouldn't. Identify who, where and what sorts of contacts you want to build and make time to create a plan with goals. Does that sound a bit odd? Perhaps. But otherwise, how are you going to manage the time to make it happen? Remember the model PIE? This stands for Performance, Image and Exposure. The further we are in our career, the less it is about competence because that is assumed, and the more it is about our Image (i.e. Personal Brand), and our Exposure (i.e. who knows us).

18. **Build relationships with headhunters and executive search.** These are the people who will bring opportunities to you if you're looking outside of your current organization. Have I said

enough times yet that leadership is a relationship business? So is getting on and getting ahead in a competitive market for talent.

19. **Take care of the physical.** Leaders who don't get enough sleep, eat the wrong food, take on board too much caffeine, drink a little too much etc. All these things don't help. They do the opposite. Look after the physical and emotional needs of your body and mind and make it a priority.

20. **Laugh often and learn from your mistakes.** Because otherwise life can be simply too hard.

Evolving as a Leader

Remember Mark Twain's quote *"the two most important days in your life are the day you are born...and the day you find out why"*. Remember Florence Rigney who had worked as a nurse for 70 years in the United States and was still there, loving it? Leaders who demonstrate Executive Presence evolve. They don't always have a singular, 'upward' trajectory. Often it's about taking steps to the left and to the right before heading on up to the top. For all of us, evolving doesn't necessarily mean getting to the top at all. It's about getting to where we were meant to be. Leaders who do this well convey Executive Presence in a way that's hard to quantify. They inspire, they engage, they ignite, they motivate and they love where they are in their professional lives. How great is that?

Chapter Nine –
Resonate Like a Leader

What is Meant by Resonate?

The New Oxford Dictionary of English[3] describes the
word 'resonate' in the following terms: 'to produce a
quality of sound that is deep, full and reverberating;
the power to evoke images, memories and emotions'.
Specifically what my research determined was that
leaders who have Executive Presence and who
'resonate' with others are quite simply able to do this:

*How you sound; how you maximize the qualities of
your voice to suit the occasion and audience; how you
convey clarity, relevance, precision and brilliance
through your verbal messages.*

What We Asked

The final section of the survey invited respondents to
reply to questions in relation to the speech of
Executive Presence. Respondents were asked to
compare the most effective and least effective leaders
they knew in relation to specific communication
patterns around pace, pitch, structure, variation in

tone, emphasis. Reminding you that one of the questions posed from the survey was:

The Speech of Executive Presence

This final section examines your views on how people with Executive Presence communicate.

When speaking, the most effective leader I know does:

- *Pace*
- *Pitch*
- *Structure*
- *Variation in tone*
- *Emphasis*

When speaking, the least effective leader I know does:

- *Pace*
- *Pitch*
- *Structure*
- *Variation in tone*
- *Emphasis*

What three things make a leader's message most compelling (indicate in order of priority)? The narrative structure for answering this question is 'most compelling', 'second' and 'third'.

- *Challenging message*
- *Passion*
- *Presented an exciting vision of the future*
- *Very relevant to the audience*
- *Interesting story*
- *Clarity of points communicated*
- *Honest appraisal of how difficult it will be to achieve*
- *Very open explanation of rationale for decision*
- *Use of visuals*
- *Tailored message to the audience*

What the Research Revealed

In terms of pace:

- 85% of respondents said the *most effective leader* they know communicated at medium pace
- 9% said fast pace
- 6% said slow pace

Flipping the question in terms of pace:

- 55% of respondents said *the least effective leader* they know communicated at fast pace

- 45% said slow pace

What this reinforces is the notion of measured delivery at a medium pace is seen as most effective.

In terms of pitch:

- 84% of respondents said the *most effective leader* they know communicated at medium pitch
- 12% said low pitch
- 4% said high pitch

Flipping the question in terms of pitch:

- 59% of respondents said *the least effective leader* they know communicated at high pitch
- 6% said medium pitch
- 35% said slow pace

Now, the key piece about this data for me is simply that professional women who may have a tendency towards a higher pitched voice need to work on lowering it in order to support being perceived as being an effective leader.

In terms of structure:

- 53% of respondents said the *most effective leader* they know had 'fairly structured' messages
- 43% said highly structured
- 4% said unstructured

Flipping the question in terms of structure:

- 84% of respondents said *the least effective leader* they know communicated in an unstructured way
- 10% said highly structured
- 6% said fairly structured

My sense (and that's all it is) is that this links to the need for clarity, brevity and precision – for which storytelling – and more of that later is a very powerful tool.

In terms of variation in tone:

- 54% of respondents said the *most effective leader* they know was 'highly expressive' vocally
- 46% said 'some variation'
- 0% said monotone

Flipping the question in terms of tone:

- 83% of respondents said *the least effective leader* they know was monotone
- 10% said highly expressive
- 7% said monotone

So it would appear that there was only a slight tendency towards a highly expressive style of communication. Essentially the point here is one of balance between being expressive - but not too much!

In terms of emphasis in vocal tone:

- 59% of respondents said the *most effective leader* they know was 'highly emphatic' vocally
- 1% said 'some emphasis'
- 40% said 'little emphasis'

Flipping the question of emphasis in vocal tone:

- 87% of respondents said *the least effective leader* they know conveyed little emphasis
- 11% said highly emphatic
- 2% said some emphasis

So, in a nutshell, the most effective leaders convey Executive Presence vocally via medium pace, medium pitch, fairly structured, highly expressive tone and highly emphatic.

In terms of which three criteria make a leader's message most compelling, respondents identified having passion, presenting an exciting vision of the future and being very relevant to the audience. It is apparent that these are all about connecting to the people they lead through their verbal messaging.

Clear, Concise Communication

Here's a story for you. In 2001, I worked for a small training organization that was invited to pitch in the USA for a global top ten brand. The Managing Director and I went to the States as one of six organizations that had a 75-minute slot to present our case, in what was a competitive pitch scenario. So far, so nothing that unusual, however, it connects with clear, concise communication, so bear with me. We were first up to present that day and – for those of you who can remember that time – one of the most common technological challenges in business back at the turn of the millennium was to be able to get one's own laptop (antiquated by today's standards) to talk to the client's data projector. This continual challenge was enough to sap your morale, confidence and will to live. Anyway, back to the pitch. We walked into the room – organized in a standard 'U-shape' and occupied by fifteen men, already dressed very similarly in button down shirts and khaki trousers, who silently watched as we got organized and set up. A kindly man approached me to do some introductions and clearly he was the host for the session. As I messed about trying to sort out leads and the distance between the data projector and the screen, as well as silently screaming at my boss who had been late arriving at the meeting (fraying my nerves to hell), he started to speak. His name was Bob and he said that he had one piece of advice for us. I will remember that moment most distinctly for a variety of different reasons. At the time, as I grappled with wires, leads and travel convertors and worried about starting late (and hence, in my mind, being out of the game before we'd started), one thought was in my head. 'And you're telling us now????????' Precisely one minute before we're due to start we're getting advice from the potential client. Anyway, I digress. His words stay true to me to this day. "Be brief, be brilliant and be done."

Being Persuasive with Language

Our language is a potent tool for persuasion and leaders who have Executive presence know exactly how to use language to influence others. One of the most powerful tools for influence that the most *brilliant* communicators have and use to be persuasive is the ability to tell great stories.

Why Storytelling?

So many reasons as to why storytelling is the language of leadership. I refer to a statistic used in the first chapter of my book. Dan Levitin's book *'The Organized Mind'*[36] states that we take in the equivalent of 175 newspapers worth of information every single day. Who's reading this and genuinely thinking, "I want more information". We've all got more than enough information to be going on with. So leaders who resonate with their colleagues and customers alike are able to stand out by telling *brilliant, memorable* stories.

When did you hear your first story? My money is on the fact that this was when you were very young and it was an experience that you loved and looked forward to in the rhythm of your day. It elicited excitement, laughter, surprise, fascination, curiosity and joy – and I'll bet there was no Excel spreadsheet in sight. Research proves that stories can be powerfully persuasive. Cultures, traditions, societies, communities and rituals have all survived through the generations due to the power of great stories.

Effective leaders are great storytellers and will use them whenever they need to build relationships, connect with customers, explain complexity, answer questions, share ideas on the spot, overcome resistance, make a presentation, sell, influence, persuade, challenge, enthuse, negotiate, motivate, delight, manage, and coach others.

If that doesn't convince you why stories, then quite simply they are quick, powerful, free, natural, refreshing, energizing, collaborative, persuasive, holistic, entertaining, moving, memorable and authentic.

Three Different Types of Story
Stories about Ourselves

Our own unique experience is awash with stories. Being an authentic leader means being able to tell a personal story when the occasion warrants it. Our unique history, experience, successes, failures, inspirations, challenges all combine to make us real and to make us human. We have a basic, human desire to connect and belong. Sharing the right story, at the right time, in the right way and with the right people can inspire and ignite those around us to go further and farther than they might have previously thought.

Stories about Other People

One of the activities of all persuasive leaders is to continually gather stories about others. The incomparable Nancy Duarte[37] has studied some of the most memorable stories that have survived and been endlessly retold through history. Her work references some of the most inspiring, moving and authentic experiences of leaders in history and retelling 'big' stories – as well as stories told to us from colleagues – is a powerful way to show relevance, connection and engagement with people within our business. It's allows us - if we don't have a relevant personal story which works – to create empathy with our audience. We can show that we relate to the experience of others and that we can 'walk in their shoes'. There is extensive scientific research that suggests that human beings are 'hardwired'[38] for empathy. In other words, the way our brain works is to closely associate with ourselves others who are close to us. We can experience (or associate and then experience) emotions that others may have experienced within the story.

Stories about Brands

So many brands by way of example; let me share a couple. 'Innocent' is a British brand success story and it is a business that makes healthy food and drinks. Their story starts in 1998 when three friends called Richard Reed, Adam Balon and Jon Wright met at university. After a snowboarding holiday they decided to stop talking about starting a business and actually get on and start one. They landed on smoothies and set up their first stall at a music festival in London. A sign above the stall read "should we give up our jobs to make these smoothies?" and people were asked to throw their empties into bins marked 'Yes' or 'No'. The bin marked 'Yes' won. After the enthusiasm and ringing customer endorsement a business plan for funding was the next hurdle. On the Innocent website[39] they describe this as the boring bit. It was re-written eleven times as every bank, venture capitalist and business angel in London turned them down.

Leveraging their network was the next step as they wrote an email entitled 'does anyone know anyone who is rich?' to every single person they knew. A wealthy investor made contact and from there, the next challenge was deciding on a name. The business started with the name 'Fast Tractor' (no, I don't get that one either), and 'Hungry Aphid' followed it. (No need for Stephen Hawking to understand why that didn't last long as a brand name). After nine months and pit stops at the names 'Nude' and 'Naked', the company settled on 'innocent'. The company started with three drinks recipes and added what it calls 'thickies' (which are yoghurt-based drinks) in 2000. Advertising, media, geographical expansion and product development followed – with a minor blip of nearly going bankrupt because the business gave over 40% of its profits to charity. As a result they set up their own charitable foundation that uses 10% of its annual profits to do good. So far they have committed over £2.4m and directly helped over 530,000 people worldwide.

In 2010, the American drinks giant, Coca Cola, came knocking and bought a 42 per cent in the business. The company continued to go from strength to strength and in 2011 announced that innocent smoothies was Europe's best selling smoothie. The following year innocent smoothies were the official smoothie and juice of the London 2012 Olympic and Paralympic Games with the launch of a special Olympic smoothie, which served drinks to visitors and athletes across the Olympic Park. Unsurprisingly the business posted record profits that year and in 2013 Coca Cola purchased the remaining 58 per cent share for a reported £65 million.

What a great story about a brand's success. A postscript too – when Innocent has AGMs, this acronym does *not* stand for Annual General Meeting. For them it's A Grown-Up Meeting. And there are many, many more that we can tell.

Isn't that fantastic?

Building a Great Story

One of the most persuasive speeches ever told was by President Abraham Lincoln. When he was voted into office it was not based on a majority, and his success at being elected only resulted from the fact that there had been four candidates vying for the presidency. Despite this inauspicious start, Lincoln built a reputation as a powerful and persuasive orator and his Gettysburg address is widely acknowledged as a powerful case study in the art and science of persuasion.

Lincoln used the power of storytelling in this address by demonstrating what all great stories have – and that is the equivalent of 'once upon a time'. His speech began with "Four score and seven years ago our fathers brought forth on this continent, a new nation, conceived in liberty, and dedicated to the proposition that all men are created equal". [40]

This opening sentence is a grown up equivalent of 'once upon a time', and what it does – as all great stories do – is indicate to the audience that what he is about to do is tell a story.

Narrative Structures

We know that all stories have a beginning, middle and an end. So far; so nothing new. The point of mentioning it is that a beginning, middle and end are what are known as a 'narrative structure'. A 'narrative structure' is quite simply a way of organising information into a format that is easy, simple and logical to follow. Anyone who has ever been on a presentation skills programme knows that presentations are divided into (a) tell them what you're going to tell them (b) tell them (c) tell them what you've told them.

The other point about narrative structures is that they are divided into *three* parts. Not seven, or five or ten parts but *three* parts. This is important because

'Three' is the most effective number into which we should divide our story (and our message. The number three has significance through history and across religion, culture, politics and business. How many wise monkeys are there? How many wise men were there? How many times did the devil allegedly tempt Jesus? In Judaism there are three patriarchs. We count to three before doing something (not four or five or six etc.). In sport, how many places are there on a medal podium? In so doing we reveal the importance of what three does; it creates a rhythm and that's what we look for in communication as human beings.

How many straplines can you think of in three parts?

- 'I'm Loving It" (McDonalds)
- "Just Do It" (Nike)
- Finger Licking' Good (KFC)
- Snap, Crackle and Pop (Rice Krispies),
- Beanz Meanz Heinz (Heinz)
- Consider It Done (UPS)
- Ford Goes Further (Ford)
- Today, Tomorrow, Toyota (Toyota)
- Taste The Rainbow (Skittles)
- Every Little Helps (Tesco)

- Never Knowingly Undersold (John Lewis)
- Imagination At Work (GE)
- Vorsprung durch Technik (Audi)
- Diamonds Are Forever (De Beers)
- We Try Harder (Avis)
- Lifts And Separates (Playtex)

And the list goes on and on and on! The point is, the most powerful messages are in three parts – and so should any story that we tell at work. I refer to my earlier story and the advice given to me to "be brief, be brilliant and be done". As a piece of advice, it's in three parts!!! And so it is with the most famous advertising straplines.

Narrative structures in business abound. Just a couple might be 'stop, start, continue'; 'problem, opportunity, action'; 'wins, learns, next steps' etc. Truly, there are hundreds. Say less and mean more, and whilst the theory is very straightforward, be under no illusion that this is a skill like any other. It takes time and practice. Otherwise the temptation (and reality) is that we waffle – miles off the point.

What all Good Stories also Have A Clear Objective

It is all too easy to underestimate the value of, and ability to identify, a clear objective. As a professional Executive Coach, one of the most challenging questions that I regularly ask my clients is 'what's your objective?' The reason why I think that this is so difficult is that on many occasions the answer I get is actually historical. It's background, context, rationale – but it's not a *goal*. Sounds easy; but in my experience this is much more difficult to do than one might imagine. Thinking in terms of outcomes, and being able to articulate clear, specific goals is not commonplace. Hence, when it comes to stories and the use of them for the purpose of influence, it is *essential* to be clear on what we want to achieve by the end of telling it.

One of my clients is a global healthcare business. Everywhere you look people are presenting to each other. When they're not presenting; they're sharing presentations or pitches with each other via email. What is the purpose of so doing? Here's my view: unless this is being done to (a) drive a decision (b) clarify action (c) gain commitment then why, why, why are we doing this? A common repost is that such PowerPoint decks are for the purposes of 'providing an update'. Why? To achieve what exactly? Who is reading this thinking: 'I don't have enough information in my life. I miss it. I need more!' I don't think so. It is entirely possible that you don't have the *right* information or the *most useful* information. However, as outlined in the first chapter, we have *more* information at our fingertips that ever before. We're overwhelmed with data at our fingertips. That's not our struggle as leaders. The point is; if we don't know what we want to achieve by sharing a presentation (or story), then that's all we're doing; sharing information.

Attention Grabbers

What else do all great stories need to have? One of my favourite books of all time begins with the line: 'Last night I dreamt I went to Manderley again.'[45] This is the opening line to the book 'Rebecca' by Daphne Du Maurier. Another life long favourite was voted the best opening line in literature in history by The Telegraph newspaper[46], which is a broadsheet newspaper in the United Kingdom. The line is: "It is a truth universally acknowledged, that a single man in possession of a good fortune, must be in want of a wife."[46] This was, of course, 'Pride and Prejudice', written by the incomparable Jane Austen in 1813. My point is that these books – and indeed any good story – has got a **'grab me by the throat'** ability. It draws us in; spikes our interest, elicits a reaction. It *engages and connects us* so that we can't wait to find out more. Consider for a moment people in your life with whom you enjoy spending time. You may find them amusing, interesting, thought provoking and many other things besides. I bet that they can do this brilliantly.

As leaders, and in the context of storytelling, this is so important because it links to an earlier point made. In practical terms, how do you grab someone's attention? Well, let's start with some underlying principles:

- Start with something unexpected. As a coping mechanism for information and processing we typically operate with what is termed 'automatic attention'. In other words, the way we process information that is expected, is typical, is 'every day', gets a level of attention that is literally at the back of our minds'. One of the things that I love about language and how we speak is that we often say what is really going on in the expressions we use. We use phrases such as 'at the back of my mind' and it is literally true in terms of where most, everyday information is processed and stored.

- Start with something that is very listener-centric. I have just finished a superb book called *The Attention Economy*[76] that argues that, more than ideas or talent; attention is the scarcest resource there is. In addition, if leaders and organizations do not act to attract, develop and protect attention then it will harm their competitiveness. In the context of telling stories this simply means making the message all about what the listener cares about. The classic acronym WIIFM (What's In It For Me) is what this is essentially looking to drive.

- Speak to the heart; not just the head. A great line from the film 'Steel Magnolias'[77] is 'the only thing that separates us from the animals is our ability to accessorize.' I would suggest a variation on that which is that the only thing that separates us from the animals is that humans have the ability to talk about how we feel. In other words, we can engage others in a story and grab their attention by talking about and connecting with emotion.

- Focus on the 'pain'[78]. Neil Rackham wrote a groundbreaking book in the world of consultative selling called 'SPIN selling'®. One of the specific tactics that successful, professional salespeople use to motivate clients to act is to focus on the problem or 'pain'. The notion being that when it comes to the psychology of influence, and what actually motivates buyers to take action, the more the problem or 'pain' is expanded, the greater grows the appetite to do something about it.

Give me some Context

Context provides the backdrop to the story that you're about to tell. In other words, why tell the story here? Why tell it now? Why tell it to us? Context answers the 'who cares right now?' question. Without the right context, we readily and quickly disengage. Storytellers always give us the backdrop so that we can create meaning and understand why we are being told this story. If we're not able to contextualize the story these are the questions that our audience will quickly be considering (and as a result), switching off – no matter how good the story is.

Metaphor and Analogy Turn Tedious, Dry, Boring Topics into Repeatable Sound Bites

Have you ever sat through a dull presentation? One

where it would be infinitely more interesting and slightly less painful to set fire to your own eyebrows? Data dense, highly technical, excruciatingly detailed, dry content is never a story. It's just a tsunami of information that will induce a coma. The point is, however, it represents a message that needs to be shared – so – our challenge is to use a story and to do so in a different way. The best tools in this instance are metaphor and analogy. In other words, tell a simple story using sports, politics, fables, religion, history, humour or any one of hundreds of facets of life to convey the message. I have a client who works in the Telco sector. They are responsible for leading a large number of projects, which are very technical and strategically important, in nature. There's a lot of technical detail that can – well – cause the listener to glaze over somewhat. One of the leaders with whom I have worked used to share PowerPoint decks of more than 35 slides (yes, I know), in font size 12 with a stunning density of information on each. (Wake up!) It was not great. The necessity of regular updates made sense but whether or not the audience's attention was captured and galvanized by what he wrote – well, let's just say, perhaps not. To prove that few people read it, his first task was to insert utterly random words like aubergine, xylophone and dodecahedron to see who noticed it and commented. No one did. So instead we turned to metaphor and analogy. The theme used to brighten up an otherwise dry and dusty story was a TV show that was a completely unexpected hit in the UK in 2014. It is called 'The Great British Bake Off'[79]. It was (and still is), an extraordinary television hit about ordinary people baking extraordinary things. It enabled my client, through the dramas of what was happening each week, plus the concept of cooking and baking in general, to use a wide variety of metaphors to provide key messages that the audience needs to understand and take decisions on, all through the use of metaphor and analogy.

If we cast our minds back through history and wonder what are some of the most famous speeches that have ever been made, then certainly some obvious candidates come to mind. Martin Luther King's 'I Have A Dream Speech' would certainly be right up there. More recently, when Steve Jobs launched the revolutionary new device (which we take for granted today) called the iPhone. Nancy Duarte[37], an academic has researched and analyzed thousands of presentations and referenced both these speeches in her written work.[37] Duarte was interested in understanding what made some presentations resonate and what made others completely flatline. What is it about putting a story into a presentation that can make it as dull as ditchwater? Duarte is a brilliant and inspirational academic whose premise was that if presentations were to have a shape – what is the shape? Her conclusion was that all great stories have a beginning (status quo), followed by a call to action where a story contrasts continually between 'what is' and 'what could be'. Her fascinating work reveals that the most powerful, moving, memorable stories move back and forth between 'what is' (in other words the current situation), and 'what could be' (in other words the ideal future scenario). **Creating a strong a** contrast between 'what is' and 'what could be' creates a tension or momentum for change. There is a cadence or rhythm to going 'back and forth' which inspires those who hear it. That's what makes the message memorable.

Finally, all great stories should have a STAR moment. STAR stands for Something They'll Always Remember. Duarte[37] coined this acronym and it's simply brilliant. The idea behind the tool is that it creates a memorable moment; a talking point; a perfect manifestation or representation of the idea behind the story. A STAR moment can be a pithy sound bite, a memorable quote, a powerful visual, facts and figures that are easy to recall (but that also surprise, shock or galvanize us – otherwise we forget them). Duarte[37] explains that a STAR moment can also be dramatic – as in when Bill Gates gave a TED talk in 2009[47] about malaria. Gates is renowned for his philanthropic work and one of his passions is obliterating malaria. Gates quoted statistics that reveal that more money is spent on research into anti-baldness drugs for men in the western world than is spent on fighting malaria in countries that are still cursed with it. He had a jam jar filled with mosquitoes, opened the top and said "there's no reason only poor people should have the experience"[47].

The Telling of a Great Story

Quite simply – it's the way we tell them. A great story can be murdered by poor delivery. Ask any actor and they'll agree. So many things to think about and as you read, you are invited, dear reader, to consider how these verbal strategies can apply in language you use when you're not telling a specific *story* by the way. In other words, these are principles of persuasive and articulate verbal communication.

Lower, Slower, Clearer

There have been a number of studies that have specifically focused on the question of pitch and leadership perception. Research published in 2012 by the University of California in San Diego[55] evaluated a sample of CEOs and found that those with deeper voices managed larger companies and made more money. What was fascinating to discover was that a 1% decrease in vocal pitch equated to a $30million increase in firm size and $19,000 higher salary. How extraordinary is that?

A different context (but relevant none the less) was research published in 2011, which suggests that when it comes to choice of partner, women remember the speaker who has a deep, low-pitch male voice. In other words, the pitch of a man's voice has a long-term impact on memory for women[56]! So, for any gentlemen reading this who might be looking for a lady friend, just take note is all I'm saying.

A further example is actually the world of the courtroom. There is an extraordinary amount of consideration behind how defendants can be perceived as more compelling, persuasive, believable and trustworthy as witnesses. Research[57] suggests that someone who sounds like James Earl Jones[58] will be perceived as more trustworthy than someone with a higher vocal pitch. Interestingly, San Diego State University published some research in January 2015[70] which was designed to test whether or not people's voices change in predictable ways when they are put in positions of power. The former UK Prime Minister Margaret Thatcher, whose voice changed extensively during the course of her political career, inspired their research. The survey was designed with two studies where students were asked to play a specific role in a negotiation exercise – one was 'high rank" and the other was "low rank" with their voices recorded. A second group, who were unaware of the construct, were able to discern (through volume and pitch of the speaker), who were the "high rank" from those of "low rank". In essence, what the research revealed was that being in a position of power can fundamentally change the way you speak and that others can pick up on these vocal cues to identify who is really 'in charge'.

As these different examples of research reflect, the context for the impact of vocal pitch is critical and there is a wide degree of variation. However, that all said, competence and the perception of trust are associated for men and women in a lower pitch, or more typically masculine, pitch to the voice.

Switching gears, let's talk about speed of vocal delivery. Rather than referencing research, let me shake it up a bit with some simple facts. Listening to you is like watching fireworks. Light travels faster than sound. When you watch fireworks, they will explode into the sky and you will register visually the experience noticeably ahead of hearing the sound of them. We need time to process what you're saying; absorb it, consider it, form an opinion on it. Talking fast is not associated with 'presence'. It's associated with haste, chaos, being disorganized and is simply not as effective. I am very aware of a number of accents that naturally speak fast. Frankly I could sit and listen to them all day and I'm not suggesting fundamentally changing the accent. What can happen when speaking fast is the amalgamation of words – so pronunciation can become less precise and that only makes being understood harder. Remember the goal here is conveying 'presence'. So, if what we're doing is making it harder to understand the message, then that's not going to work. Quite simply for those times and for those messages where you want to convey confidence, authority and poise then the best approach is *just slow down.*

The Power of the Pause

Have you ever watched a Woody Allen film[59]? Like him or loathe him, his films beautifully demonstrate the impact of emotion on speech. His characters speak at an ever-faster pace as the story unfolds and at points, can sound frankly unintelligible. One of the first techniques public speakers learn is the power of the pause. Being able to 'hold' your audience in silence as they wait, in expectation, for what you want to say next is a superb representation of exquisite influence. Leaders with presence are able to do so without fear of interruption. That's influence. So, how do we do it in a way that achieves this…rather than communicating the impression that you don't know what you are talking about and are actually in a minor mental meltdown? Natalie Bennett[60,] take note. For those of you currently wondering if she was the chick in 'Pride and Prejudice'[61]; well, all I can say is not quite. Bennett is a politician and Leader of the Green Party who was interviewed on a UK radio channel during the build up to the UK election of May 2015. I've referenced the link to the audio so that you can always listen for yourselves. It's painful and not what I'm talking about in relation to the use of pause for impact.

The pause can be used in two ways. Firstly, as a mechanism to increase anticipation, interest, excitement at a critical point in your message. So, an example might be: "if there's only one thing you need to take away from this presentation in order to be successful (pause) it's this". Alternatively, using the pause as a means to allow reflection after a key fact is another highly effective use. For example, "President Abraham Lincoln was the only US President who was also a licensed bar tender". Pausing after this (it's an example people, I fully realise you're not likely to be running out to share this statistic any time soon), will allow the listener to absorb what you say and take in the enormity and relevance of it.

High Rising Terminals (HRT)

I thought that the acronym HRT could only mean one thing, until I started coaching vocal impact. There is a description of language that is called a high-rising terminal (HRT), and it is also known as an 'Australian Question Intonation' (AQI). Another label is 'up-talk' and it is the act of raising the intonation or pitch of the voice at the end of a sentence, such that makes the statement sound like a question and is common in Australian and American accents. There has been a great deal of discussion about high rising terminals in the last few years in the US, with Kim Kardashian and Lena Dunham - when acting in TV comedy Girls[62] - cited as examples. In the UK, it is garnering a great deal of negative press[63], and there is a school of thought which says the HRT gained traction in this country when the Australian soap 'Neighbours'[64] appeared on our screens in 1986.

So what is the implication if speaking with a high rising terminal in a business context? The publishing company Pearson polled 700 male and female managers about the trend of young Britons using 'Australian Question Intonation' as part of book being published called 'Speak For Yourself'[65]. The survey audience was a mixture of professionals in managerial, executive and ownership roles. Interestingly, results revealed that 57% believed that speaking with an AQI or HRT has the capability to damage a person's professional credibility[66], because it conveys a reluctance to speak their mind. In addition, 70% of respondents said the inflections are 'annoying', while 85% said that when non-Australian people speak this way it is a 'clear indicator' of insecurity or emotional weakness and could hinder their chances of a promotion. Only 16% were willing to overlook this vocal habit to focus purely on their capability for the role. The audience where this prevalence for speaking has grown most is amongst teenagers and graduates.

However, my thoughts are there as a cultural context at play. In other words, in Australia, New Zealand and the United States, the upward inflection is generally fine (as long as it's not excessive), but in Western Europe and from a perspective of conveying presence; it simply doesn't work at all – unless it is an occasion where you want to pose a question.

Fillers - Otherwise Known as the 'Sentence Stuffer' or a 'Rubbish' Word

Fillers are words (or sounds) that we use as a way to stall for time when speaking and historically have used them. "It has nothing to do with sloppiness", says John Ayto, editor of the Oxford Dictionary of Modern Slang[67]. "It is not a lazy use of language, that is a common fallacy among non-linguists,"[68] he says. "We all use fillers because we can't keep up highly-monitored, highly-grammatical language all the time. We all have to pause and think."[68] Of course he is right; and there is a context for talking about 'fillers'. Firstly, when we need to convey confidence, authority, certainty, we need to reduce fillers because it can communicate the exact opposite of that which we are trying to convey. Secondly, it can be a 'verbal crutch' on which we anchor the rest of our messaging. In other words, what happens is that we can easily form the habit of using the word throughout our speech and for the audience – be it formal or informal – they become fixated on the word and start counting it, thereby deleting the rest of the message.

Knowing when to Stop Talking

How can you tell if you tend to talk too much? A great article that I read recently[69] suggests that there are four signs that should give you a clue if you're perceived at work as a windbag. They are:

- **People look at their phones or screens rather than at you.** This is a quite obvious (and quite brutal) non-verbal communication to indicate that they are absorbed in something else, which for them holds a higher priority or merit.
- **People are locked into earplugs.** That's an even more overt signal that I can totally ignore it.
- **You do most of the talking.** This one is a personal bugbear of mine in a social setting. I remain extraordinarily surprised by the number of well-educated, decent people who appear on meeting to love the sound of their own voices and just 'transmit'. No questions or interest shown in others; it's just 'all about me.com'.
- **Your answers to a question are never concise.** Sometimes a question deserves a concise answer. If in doubt of *how not to do it;* listen to any political interview. Their answers are lengthy, often not connected to the question posed, and designed to take the questioner off in a different direction. That may (or may not) be okay for political interviews, but it certainly is not in business.

Generally speaking, if they look like they are trying to find a quick, painless death then you are the cause. Stop talking and ideally go away. Or learn how to 'be brief, be brilliant and be done'.

Be Brief, Be Brilliant And Be Done

Say less and achieve more.

Avoid Sharing Internal Dialogue

Internal dialogue is quite simply the conversations and things that we say to ourselves. We 'hear' what we say and it's our thinking process that's going on out loud, in our head. The most conversations we have in our life are with ourselves and we have thousands of these *every day*. If you know someone, who happen to be that person yourself, who 'speaks to themselves', then this is simply articulating your internal dialogue. Anyway, what's the point of this? Well, at a psychological level, our internal dialogue has a profound impact on what we say about anything, so it's important. However, in this specific context what I am referring to is the notion of *not* sharing your processing along with your point of view. Here's an example. If you were asked the question 'what's your favourite television programme?' a crisp and concise answer would be (for me) 'The West Wing'.[19] If, however, I was prone to sharing my internal dialogue then my answer might sound something like this: 'well, it depends because gosh, I don't know, there are lots of programmes I really like. I've been re-watching 'The West Wing' recently which I love, but then I also really like 'Veep'[165] as well. So, on balance I think I'd say it would be 'The West Wing'." The latter example of an answer reveals our mental processing. That wasn't required. It's cluttered, lengthier with the potential to be irritating. A far more persuasive and poised answer would be to pause (the beauty of which is well known), and then answer – concisely.

Language that Resonates

In Chapter One I focused on the necessity of this conversation. In other words, the necessity of leaders to focus on 'Executive Presence'. The reality is that now more than ever, leaders need to understand how to persuade, motivate, enthuse and garner support like never before. And they need the language to match. Businesses today (with one or two specific industry exceptions) do not have the command and control structures of yesteryear. The dreaded 'matrix' organization of dotted lines and cross functional teams with much flatter structures is the new norm and fundamentally full of people with their arms folded saying 'why should I do that then?' Hence our language *has to* resonate, persuade, overcome objection, galvanize and motivate others to support our point of view, take action on our behalf, give us money from their budgets and so on.

State Things that People want to Agree With

The psychology of persuasion says that when we state things that people want to agree with (an example might be – we want to make sure the work is fairly distributed, or, we need to make sure everyone is heard etc.), by including this in our language this is very effective in persuading others to our point of view. In the world of Neuro Linguistic Programming (or NLP for short), there is a very effective strategy called 'pacing and leading'. Funnily enough it's in three parts and quite simply involves pacing (which means acknowledging the other person's perspective) once, followed by pacing again (stating something which appreciates the other point of view for a second time) followed by leading (asserting our own point of view or making a suggestion). This approach is highly persuasive because it shows acknowledgement, (but not necessarily agreement) with the opinion of others and that's critical for them to feel heard and validated. Without this, and by simply stating what we think, we may not persuade at all – we just sound like we disagreeing.

Use 'Our', 'We' and 'Us' rather than 'You, 'I' and 'Me'

The use of 'our' versus 'I' has been found to be consistently more effective. James Pennebaker wrote a fantastic book called *The Secret Life Of Pronouns*[41] in which (amongst many glorious insights), Pennebaker suggests that individuals of higher status use more first person plural pronouns (e.g. our, we, us) and make much less use the first person singular 'I' pronoun. This language suggests a more inclusive, collaborative, 'we're all in this together' type of style.

Because, Because, Because, Because

'Because of the wonderful things he does' is the line from the Wizard of Oz[42]. The Huffington Post[43] published a fabulous article in December 2014 that explored the most persuasive words in the English language. The word 'because' has been shown to be highly persuasive in getting others to do our bidding. The article references the work of Ellen Langer[44], who was a Harvard University psychologist who conducted a famous study about a photocopier and how to jump the queue. The original study was done in the 1970s (important to note given the example used which is dated as a construct even if the result still holds true). Langer's research showed that when she tried to jump the queue, (or cut in line for our international audience who don't exactly understand what's just been written); one word could make a powerful difference to her success rate. Specifically, what Langer found was that when she asked: "Excuse me, I have five pages. May I use the Xerox machine?" her success rate was 60%. When she became more specific by saying "Excuse me, I have five pages. May I use the Xerox machine because I am in a rush?" the success rate increased to 94 per cent.

However, when she said "Excuse me, I have five pages. May I use the Xerox machine because I have to make some copies', the success rate remained unchanged, even when the reason had been removed. In other words, it was the word 'because' that was so powerful.

Affirmative Language

The power and beauty of affirmative language is that it describes exactly what you expect to happen. It asserts that a fact is true. For example, if you say '*when* this project is finished, we will be able to sell more product'. It assumes a certain response or conclusion and this is so much more influential than saying "*if* you finish the project, we will be able to see more product'.

Assertive Language

Assertive language is where we are able to be confident and direct in stating our views, requests or requirements. So for example, saying 'I *need* three more weeks to fulfil your requirements'. This is very different (and more influential) than saying 'I *guess* that about three more weeks would help me to fulfil your requirements'. This is much more confident and persuasive to hear.

Things Great Leaders Never Say

I was curious to understand some of those 'you are not serious…really?' words or phrases that any effective leader should just *remove, delete, destroy* from their vocabulary. Here are some of them:

"I Don't Care" There are so many levels at which this can be misconstrued. Fundamentally, if we don't care, then we cannot expect our people to. If we don't care about them, engagement plummets and so does performance. When we're frustrated, saying 'I don't care' is incredibly dismissive. Your people won't forget it if you do.

"I'm The Boss" Margaret Thatcher once said, "Power is like being a lady. If you have to tell people you are, you aren't."[48] A favourite expression of mine is 'self praise is no praise'. Again, like Thatcher suggests, if you have to remind people of your strengths, then perhaps those strengths are not quite as strong as you thought. Leaders need to be authentically acknowledging the talent of others, rather than reminding the rest of us about themselves.

"That's Not My Fault" Leadership is not about pointing the finger of blame all the time. Ultimately leadership is about responsibility and galvanizing people around us to find and make a solution work. Humility and accountability is a leader's lot and emotional intelligence says that we need to be comfortable to own it when things go wrong. It's a powerful way to get others around you to help fix it.

"Failure Is Not An Option" When you stand back from this sentence it really is absurd. We learn from mistakes and any skill we've ever learned has been learned by making boatloads of mistakes to understand how to execute that skill more effectively. As Ariana Huffington has been quoted as saying, 'failure is not the opposite of success; it's part of success'[49]. It also says everything about the culture of a business. In other words, failure is not allowed.

Well, that's not going to build the kind of engagement you need from your colleagues and team if that's the mentality that is adopted.

"That's Not How We Do Things Around Here"
There are a number clients with whom I am currently working where our focus is *the language of innovative* leadership. Whilst conducting research for this book (and for the work I'm doing with these clients), it would be remiss not to talk about Steve Jobs. Amongst some of his most memorable quotes is this: "innovation distinguishes between a leader and a follower"[50]. So leaders who say: "that's not how we do things around here" are at risk of creating a culture where we do what we've always done; and don't challenge the status quo.

"I'll Do It" The higher up the business you are; the more your role is to help others deliver and excel; rather than suffering from the 'over contributor' syndrome. I've seen too many good businesses fail to grow and fulfil their potential due to the owner suffering from the 'saviour syndrome'. Leaders need to nurture the talent of others, rather than suffer from the delusion that things are best done by them. As a client once said to me: "you don't have a dog and bark yourself". How true that is, but more than that, leadership is fundamentally about driving performance through others. So, even if you could do it, why on earth would you always want to?

"I had a great year/quarter/month/performance"
Back to the glorious James Pennebaker and his book *The Secret Life Of Pronouns*[41]. The point about

leadership is that it's not 'all about me.com'. It's all about our people. *We* had a great performance this month, *we* had a great quarter, *and we* had a great year. Forget this at your peril.

Things Great Leaders Always Say Congratulations

Authentic, well-earned, enthusiastic appreciation of something positive (whether it's professional or personal) moves us. Given the pace, challenge and change within our daily working lives, it allows a rare moment to celebrate, appreciate and recognize something positive. Who honestly has had their fill of it? Who genuinely thinks reading this that they are replete when it comes to being congratulated? So, why would we think our team thinks any different?

What Are We Doing Well And How Can We Do More Of It?

One of the challenges as a leader is to find the space to focus on what's going well within the business. When there is a lot of change, when the commercial challenge is great, when times are tough, the easiest (and most understandable) thing to do is to focus on the problems. Think about this in the context of performance. When we look at our numbers, *it's very easy to focus on where we are off the pace.* However, when there's a lot to improve, this can become quite demoralising. Chip and Dan Heath consider this concept in their book '*Switch – How To Change Things When Change Is Hard*'[51]. Effectively one of the concepts that they reference is 'bright spots'. These are small glimmers of things that are working well and they challenge the norm of ignoring these. As a leader we need to **investigate success with even greater curiosity than we investigate failure**.

Thank you

It may sound petty; but how often do we make time to properly and sincerely thank our people for a job well done? In 2013, Glassdoor[52] published an Employee Appreciation Survey, which was conducted online by Harris Interactive on behalf of Glassdoor[52]. Amongst a sample of 2,044 workers, 53% of employees would stay at their company longer if they felt more appreciation from their boss. In addition, 81% said they're motivated to work harder when their boss shows appreciation for their work. Quite simply the question I would pose is this: who amongst you currently feels full to the brim of appreciation for the work that you do? Almost no one will say 'yes'. So, what on earth makes us think that our team feels any different? Authentic, relevant appreciation for a job well done is one of the most powerful and regular things that we can say to drive greater engagement and productivity from our team.

How Are You? (And Mean It)

A cross-cultural consideration is needed here. Our American friends use 'How are you?' as a greeting and it's like saying 'hi' or 'hello'. In other words, they are not being unkind or thoughtless in that context, it's just an acknowledgement and they are not really after an in depth answer. So, when listing this here as something that great leaders say, I don't mean asking the question in that context. What I do mean is making time to regularly and sincerely inquire about your people. What's going on for them? As leaders our job is quite simply to drive results through others. That rarely happens without significant emotional commitment to not just the task and the company

What Do You Need?

Asking what others need is powerful because it shows that you care and that you want them to be successful. Crucially, it also shows humility and empowerment because the premise *isn't* that you have all the answers. Involving others only engages and connects them further.

What's The Story?

This is so simple. Show curiosity. What are their views, opinions and perspectives? Stephen Covey's fifth habit[53] is to 'seek first to understand before being understood'. Covey reminds us all that we're not taught to listen; we're taught to read, write and speak.

Listening sincerely and authentically is an enormous challenge in business – and never more so with the barrage of technology at our fingertips. Finding out what is really going on before launching in with our ideas and suggestions (no matter how well intended), is the only way to go.

What Can I Do To Help?

How many times have you been asked that in the last month? Telling and directing is all very well and entirely necessary, and it's not about getting into execution in a way that's not required. It's about being genuinely willing to get involved in a way that's helpful.

This Is The Story

I have talked about storytelling at length elsewhere in this chapter. Naturally as a leader we want to tell people what's going on. Structuring our messages in a way that allows clarity of understanding and action is not only logical, but if it's wrapped around a great story then it connects and engages people behind your purpose. In the absence of clarity we fill in the gaps ourselves. Lack of clarity drives lower productivity and engagement.

How Do We Move Forward?

One of the issues as a leader is to be an energizer. I don't mean naïve or inauthentic in the face of appalling tragedy. However, most situations are thankfully not like that. What I do mean is focusing (and encouraging others to do so) on what we *can do*; rather than staying forever stuck on those that we *cannot change.*

We Can All Do Better

If we never thank and appreciate people and if we never focus on 'bright spots'[51] then continually saying 'we can do better' will ultimately become decreasingly effective. If you don't add that crucial word of 'all' (so that means us as well), then it can quickly grate in terms of being about others not leaning in enough. When your team is failing; so are you. I have worked in teams where the leader believed that if we failed it was 'our' fault. He had nothing to do with it. One of the most crucial parts of leadership is to drive your team to achieve a higher standard than they themselves might think is possible. We have to congratulate them when success is achieved, of course; and be candid when they fall short of their potential. And you as the leader need to commit to finding out what you can do better. 'Us' and 'Them' in leadership doesn't exist.

It's Time to Talk about the F Word

Since we're talking about what great leaders do and do not say, let's talk about the F word. Feedback. Who amongst you genuinely feels that they receive enough feedback on their performance on a regular basis? Most professionals – no matter how senior – fail to indicate that they do. My point is that if we are to resonate as leaders, then this behaviour is a critical part of our verbal skill set. And boy, is it easy to demoralise and deflate based on our language. How do you feel when someone says: "I'd like to give you some feedback?" Usually it's a signal for the heart to sink, the eyes to water and morale to take one, big, mighty fall. Too many leaders are poor at this. Why? Who knows; but perhaps a lack of understanding regarding its purpose; a focus on themselves rather than the person receiving it; a poor structure and little practice might all have something to do with it. I left a company based on the appalling way in which my boss gave feedback.

How to Give Good Feedback

Leaders who resonate will provide feedback as part of their operational rhythm. And, it's not always negative! They build a culture where individuals crave it and challenge the organization when they're not receiving enough feedback – be it positive or otherwise – to help them in their role. The purpose of feedback is to help the individual feel helped; not harmed. It shouldn't be a surprise; it should be objective with clear, clean language describing the impact of what was observed with a recommendation for what is required in the future. In the case of positive feedback, it may be as simple as 'more of the same, please'. Anyone giving feedback needs to own it; not distance themselves from it. In other words, vague references such as "there is a feeling that...." or "it may be that on occasion others sense that etc." These are just by way of example. My point is that if you give feedback; it should be yours to own. Otherwise the receiver of said wisdom will quickly be confused by what you say and unable to ask questions to clarify what does and what does not work about their behaviour. It's not that they want to ask, "who said that?" (And if they did; the absolute worst thing to say is 'I can't tell you". Good luck with building an open, collaborative culture after that.) In addition, it does nothing to build trust and co-operation between team members because the implication is that there are 'closed door' conversations going on about you. Let's be grown up about this.

And can we please, please, please make time to regularly give feedback on what is working? A 'well done' or a 'thank you' is lovely; but it's essential to make time to regularly provide positive, genuinely deserved feedback. They've earned it and so they should have it. I distinguish between praise and feedback using the following metaphor. Praise is like a pat on the back (very nice but very fleeting), whereas positive feedback - if well structured and thought through - is the equivalent of a lovely long stroke. Much more enjoyable and it lasts much longer.

I have talked elsewhere in this book about the concept of 'bright spots'[51] and as leaders, we have to investigate success with even more curiosity than we investigate failure. If leaders genuinely want to harness their talent, drive engagement and deliver for the business this is a critical area that is easily ignored, poorly executed and potentially catastrophic for teams if we don't get right.

There are plenty of models to use to structure feedback: AID (Action, Impact, Desired Outcome) or Likes, Concerns, Suggestions are as good as any. Personally I'm not a fan of the feedback sandwich (i.e. here's something done well; here's something to change and finally here's something done well again). It earned a more Anglo-Saxon name in recent years, and perhaps rightly so as over use and a lack of sincerity caused recipients of said feedback to think that it was all a load of nonsense. As you can probably tell, I'm not a fan. As a leader I think we can inspire, engage, excite and delight our people through the language of providing feedback, simply by giving it a bit more thought, a more authentic structure and some regular use.

Finally, make time to practise this and don't resort to email to do so.

Chairmanship Skills

A fantastic piece of research that I have used for years is based on the work of Neil Rackham and Peter Honey[153.]It is based on the work of negotiation and reveals the number of misunderstandings that two individuals will have *if they fail to use some of these strategies,* for each and every hour that they are together. These techniques are powerful, not just for negotiation, but also facilitation and whether the audience is large or small, can enhance the quality of both the discussion and the output.

Making Suggestions (for Content or Procedure)

Have you ever been in a conversation or meeting that appears to be going around in circles? People who like the sound of their own voice, or who lack clarity in terms of the direction of the conversation, or who may simply be 'stuck' surround you and yet it feels as if there is no way out? One approach is to make a suggestion – either for content or process. What I mean by that, for example, is to suggest that we talk about the budget or we talk about the people or we talk about the agenda. In other words you make a suggestion about the topic or content for the discussion. The alternative approach is to make a suggestion about process. For example, let's talk about the budget followed by the people and then finish by talking about the awards ceremony. So you are laying out an agenda and order for the discussion.

It can 'unstick' a conversation, maintain neutrality but help move things forward and is a powerful verbal tool.

Building

This approach quite simply means adding to the comment or suggestion of others – hence 'building' on it. The point is, not to change the original comment but to augment it. Beware of repetition – don't repeat what the other person has said – because that becomes irritating very quickly.

Supporting

This simply does what it says on the tin. It's a verbal demonstration of agreement with someone else. A simple example: "I agree with John".

Signposting

This is where we state what is going to happen next. An example might be: 'I have a question'. This means that what follows is…a question. Or, 'I need to summarise my understanding,' which means that what will follow is….a summary of my understanding. The impact of verbal signposting is that it does two things: (a) it demonstrates high self awareness by describing the behavior that you are about to complete and (b) it is a 'smoother' landing into a conversation and so is perceived as assertive without being perceived as aggressive.

Bringing in/Shutting out

This is simply about inviting others to enter the conversation or preventing them from doing so at a particular moment. For example, if we were to say: "Bob, what are your thoughts on the topic we've been discussing?" This is a way of bringing in Bob to the conversation. Equally, if we were to say: "Bob, we'd like to hear from John first", then that is a way of shutting him out until after John has spoken.

Testing Understanding

This is simply where we provide a verbal signpost that informs others of the need to check what we have heard and/or discussed. For example: "let me check that I've understood what you're saying. Is it blah, blah, blah?"

Summarizing

Another one of those 'does exactly what it says on the tin'. The point of a summary is to condense what's been said and create a pivot point – so it is a chance to then switch the conversation in a different direction or start to draw it to a conclusion.

The Cross Cultural Context

There are many professionals who focus on cross-cultural communication and know much more than I on this topic. The message is simple; leaders who fail to consider the impact of their communication when working with a multi-national workforce are making a perilously naïve mistake. What we say and what we mean, no matter our culture, is a complex, nuanced subject. So, doing the research, listening and seeking to understand what the norms, practicalities and considerations are in order to reach out and connect with others are simply *essential*. To prove the point, I thank The Idealist Revolution[105] for the following:

What People Say and What They Actually Mean[105]

1. **'I might join you later'** — Translation: I'm not leaving the house today unless it's on fire.

2. **'Excuse me, sorry, is anyone sitting here?'** — Translation: You have three seconds to move your bag before I get really annoyed.

3. **'Not to worry.'** — Translation: I will never forget this!

4. Saying **'Sorry'** as a way of introducing yourself.

5. **'Bit wet out there.'** — Translation: You're going to need a snorkel because it's absolutely chucking it down out there!

6. Ending an email with **'Thanks'**. — Translation: I'm perilously close to losing my temper!

7. **'Right then, I really should start to think about possibly making a move.'** — Translation: Bye!

8. **'It's fine.'** — Translation: It really couldn't get any worse, but it probably will do...

9. **'Perfect.'** — Translation: Well that's ruined then!

10. **'A bit of a pickle.'** — Translation: A catastrophically bad situation with potentially fatal consequences.

11. 11: **'Not too bad, actually.'** — Translation: I'm probably the happiest I've ever been.

12. **'Honestly, it doesn't matter.'** — Translation: Nothing has ever mattered more than this.

13. **'You've caught the sun.'** — Translation: You look like you've been swimming in a volcano.

14. **'That's certainly one way of looking at it.'** — Translation: That's certainly the wrong way of looking at it.

15. Saying **'I have the 5p if it helps.'** and never knowing if it ever does help.

16. **'If you say so.'** — Translation: I'm afraid that what you're saying is the height of idiocy.

17. **'With all due respect...'** — Translation: You have absolutely no idea what you're talking about.

18. Saying **'You're welcome'** as quietly as possible to people that don't say thank you, but using it as a form of punishment.

19. Meanings of **'I beg your pardon'** — Translation: a) I didn't hear you; b) I apologize; c) What you're saying is making me absolutely livid!

20. **'It could be worse.'** — Translation: It couldn't possibly be any worse.

21. **'Each to their own.'** — Translation: You're wrong, but never mind.

22. **'Pop around anytime.'** — Translation: Please stay away from my house.

23. **'I'm just popping out for lunch, does anyone else want anything?'** — Translation: I'm getting my own lunch now; please don't ask me to get you anything!

24. Saying: **'I might get some cash out, actually'**, despite approaching the cash machine and being 100% certain of getting some cash out.

25. **'No, no, honestly it was my fault.'** — Translation: It was absolutely your fault and we both know it!

26. **'No, yeah, that's very interesting!'** — Translation: You are boring me to death!

27. **'No harm done.'** — Translation: You have ruined everything!

28. **'Just whenever you get a minute...'** — Translation: Now!

29. **'I'm sure it'll be fine.'** — Translation: I fully expect the situation to deteriorate rapidly!

30. **'Sorry, I think you might have dropped something...'** — Translation: You have definitely dropped that specific item!

A footnote to this section is an amusing personal story that made me laugh like a drain. Whilst writing this book I have shared certain sections with my husband and on revealing this particular piece of research, he obliged with the following tale. In his office is a fabulous gentleman called Kevin who hails from Barbados and who spends approximately one week a month in the United Kingdom (they are all self-employed financial advisors). One day, my husband got up from his desk and announced that he was off to a local coffee shop to buy a cappuccino and he enquired if anyone wanted anything. By way of reply, Kevin provided a list of food shopping items and asked Anthony if he wouldn't mind dropping off some clothes at the dry cleaners. Now, being the smart, intelligent, articulate and confident British man that he is, my husband said absolutely nothing and headed out to complete these tasks (with Kevin's dirty clothes and a shopping list in hand). My husband only wanted a cappuccino and he was only offering to be polite. What we say and what we mean are so extraordinarily different sometimes. So to reiterate, whilst this whole chapter has been exploring the practical strategies behind conveying presence through 'resonance', make no mistake that it is essential to consider the cross-

cultural context. I, meanwhile, need to go and track
down said husband, and finalize a joke about being
taken to the dry cleaners.

Bibliography

Chapter 1

54   http://www.mckinsey.com/insights/leading_in_the_21st_century/
decoding_leadership_what_really_matters

36   http://www.daniellevitin.com/theorganizedmind/

73   http://www.motivateus.com/leadership-quotes-for-executives.htm

110   http://gladwell.com/blink/why-do-we-love-tall-men/

134   http://www.druckerinstitute.com/peter-druckers-life-and-legacy/

156   https://hbr.org/2000/05/cracking-the-code-of-change/ar/1

157   https://www.gov.uk/government/organisations/home-office

Chapter 3

3   The New Oxford Dictionary of English, Oxford University Press, 2001.

114   http://www.oxforddictionaries.com/definition/english/charisma

150   http://www.amazon.co.uk/The-One-Minute-Manager-
Productivity/dp/0007107927

111   http://greenpeakpartners.com/

104   http://www.forbes.com/sites/victorlipman/2013/11/18/all-successful-
leaders-need-this-quality-self-awareness/

112   http://www.amazon.co.uk/Emotional-Intelligence-Matter-More-
Than/dp/0747528306

113   http://www.amazon.co.uk/dp/142212312X

115   http://www.amazon.com/The-Secret-Great-Leaders-
Know/dp/1565119444

116   http://dictionary.reference.com/browse/integrity

117   http://www.amazon.co.uk/The-Leadership-Challenge-Extraordinary-
Organizations/dp/0470651725

158   https://hbr.org/2014/05/the-best-leaders-are-humble-leaders/

159   http://www.thepaulagcompany.com/

160   http://www.tv.com/shows/miami-vice/

Chapter 4

110   http://gladwell.com/blink/why-do-we-love-tall-men/

71   Journal of Experimental Social Psychology July 2012, Vol.48 (4) 918-925; Hajo Adam and Adam D. Galinksy

72   http://www.sciencealert.com/research-shows-wearing-a-suit-changes-the-way-you-think

10   http://abcnews.go.com/US/social-media-explodes-president-obamas-tan-suit/story?id=25166551

11   http://talkingpointsmemo.com/livewire/president-obama-peter-king-tan-suit-rant

144   http://www.dailymail.co.uk/news/article-2936484/The-laidback-approach-Greece-s-new-Essex-educated-finance-minister-arrives-talks-George-Osborne-leather-jacket-minus-tie.html

1   http://www.telegraph.co.uk/men/fashion-and-style/11480176/Budget-2015-Twitter-reacts-to-George-Osbornes-strangely-cut-suit.html

2   http://www.telegraph.co.uk/men/fashion-and-style/11482554/How-to-avoid-George-Osbornes-Budget-fashion-fail.html

9   http://www.dailymail.co.uk/news/article-3013881/So-gravitas-portrait-oh-chic-Newsnight-presenter-Emily-Maitlis-spotty-tie-waistcoat-rolled-sleeves-outfit-raises-eyebrows.html

126   http://www.brainyquote.com/quotes/quotes/d/dollyparto446782.html

127   http://thebestfashionblog.com/wp-content/uploads/2012/02/Celebrities-Famous-Style-of-Clothing-1-600x918.jpg

128   http://www.forbes.com/profile/mark-zuckerberg/

129   http://nyulocal.com/wp-content/uploads/2014/02/annawintour_getty_650145a1.jpg

130   http://www.theguardian.com/fashion/2012/apr/23/why-simon-cowell-limited-wardrobe

131   http://www.dailymail.co.uk/home/moslive/article-1260422/MARTIN-BELL-Beware-newsmen-wearing-lip-gloss.html

3   The New Oxford Dictionary of English, Oxford University Press, 2001.

4   The Collins English Dictionary, Harper Collins.

5   Conselle L.C. Institute of Image Management, 2000.

109   http://www.phrases.org.uk/meanings/120300.html

121   http://www.ctshirts.co.uk/mens-shoes/view-all/Black-compton-brogue-monk-shoes?q=gbpdefault%7C%7Cml188blk%7C%7C%7C%7C%7C%7C%7C%7C%7C%7C%7C%7C%7C%7C%7C7C

122 http://www.ctshirts.co.uk/Black-Calf-Leather-Oxford-Semi--Brogues?q=gbpdefault%7C%7CML063BLK%7C%7C%7C%7C%7C%7C%7C7C%7C7C%7C7C%7C7C%7C7C%7C7C%7C7C

123 http://www.ctshirts.co.uk/mens-shoes/Black-Lansdowne-work-trainers?q=gbpdefault%7C%7CCml030blk%7C%7C%7C%7C%7C%7C%7C7C%7C7C%7C7C%7C7C%7C7C%7C7C%7C7C

124 http://www.frenchsole.com/products/view/BAB09

125 http://www.fatface.com/footwear/flip-flops/icat/womensflipflops?gclid=Cj0KEQjwkIurBRDwoZfi1bGCxocB
EiQAmcs-egvxor3ySBBNUmLlF4-lZDP38_JaiSF0garg_6kCsjYaApTA8P8HAQ

8 http://www.dailymail.co.uk/femail/article-2536442/A-QUARTER-men-wear-ill-fitting-clothes-no-idea-size-really-are.html

11 http://talkingpointsmemo.com/livewire/president-obama-peter-king-tan-suit-rant

118 http://www.huffingtonpost.com/2011/09/13/effect-of-color-red_n_959189.html

6 https://au.news.yahoo.com/a/26693750/penis-shaped-neckline-sparks-social-media-frenzy/

161 http://www.bbc.co.uk/programmes/b006mk25

162 https://en.wikipedia.org/wiki/Category:Television_series_by_
Spelling_Television

163 http://www.amazon.co.uk/John-Molloys-New-Dress-Success/dp/0446385522/ref=sr_1_1?ie=UTF8&qid=1434646322&sr=8-1&keywords=john+t+molloy+dress+for+success

164 http://lengstorf.com/travel-essentials-uniform/

Chapter 5

3 The New Oxford Dictionary of English, Oxford University Press, 2001.

12 http://www.officevibe.com/blog/disturbing-employee-engagement-infographic

13 http://www.orcinternational.com/

14 https://hbr.org/2008/07/putting-the-service-profit-chain-to-work

20 http://www.cityam.com/213121/end-sight-enron-scandal-administration-europe-ends

26 http://www.telegraph.co.uk/finance/financialcrisis/6173145/The-collapse-of-Lehman-Brothers.html

21 http://www.forbes.com/lists/2005/54/JQQC.html

22   http://www.express.co.uk/news/uk/5979/BP-Chief-quits-in-rent-boy-scandal

23   http://www.nytimes.com/2006/02/21/business/21radio.html

24   http://www.nytimes.com/2014/03/12/books/cycle-of-lies-details-the-fall-of-lance-armstrong.html

33   http://mg.co.za/article/2012-05-30-the-sullied-hero-who-died-young

34   http://news.bbc.co.uk/1/hi/sport/cricket/791890.stm

145 http://en.wikipedia.org/wiki/Jim'll_Fix_It

25   http://www.mirror.co.uk/all-about/jimmy-savile

27   http://www.huffingtonpost.co.uk/2014/07/24/catholic-sex-abuse_n_5616282.html

28   http://www.dailymail.co.uk/news/article-2661932/Revealed-John-Edwards-confessed-notorious-affair-daughter-family-home-cancer-stricken-wife-Elizabeth-house.html

29   http://abcnews.go.com/Politics/john-edwards-retried-campaign-finance-charges/story?id=16561020

30   http://michaelhyatt.com/10-mistakes-leaders-should-avoid-at-all-costs.html

31   http://www.amazon.com/Lead-Purpose-Giving-Organization-Believe/dp/0814436609

32   http://www.amazon.co.uk/Start-With-Why-Leaders-Everyone/dp/0241958229

35   http://www.amazon.co.uk/Daring-Greatly-Courage-Vulnerable-Transforms/dp/0670923540

146 http://www.amazon.co.uk/Leadership-Self-Deception-Getting-out-Box/dp/0141030062

154 http://www.nytimes.com/2014/02/23/opinion/sunday/friedman-how-to-get-a-job-at-google.html?_r=0

155 http://asq.sagepub.com/content/59/1/34.full.pdf+html

74   http://www.selfhelpdaily.com/quotes-by-ronald-reagan/

119 https://www.youtube.com/watch?v=Ks-_Mh1QhMc

147 http://www.amazon.co.uk/Working-Emotional-Intelligence-Daniel-Goleman/dp/0747543844/ref=sr_1_3?ie=UTF8&qid=1433871206&sr=8-3&keywords=daniel+goleman+emotional+intelligence

148 https://www.psychologytoday.com/basics/emotional-intelligence

149 http://www.cas.udel.edu/uas/faculty-resources/Documents/Spring%202012%20Newsletter%20I.pdf

Chapter 6

3 The New Oxford Dictionary of English, Oxford University Press, 2001.

15 http://www.amazon.com/Lions-Dont-Need-Roar-Leadership/dp/0446516678

16 http://jimcanterucci.com/powerful-leaders-active-listeners

17 https://www.stephencovey.com/7habits/7habits-habit1.php

18 http://www.amazon.co.uk/Effective-Executive-Classic-Drucker-Collection/dp/0750685077

92 http://www.ted.com/talks/amy_cuddy_your_body_language_shapes_who_you_are?language=en

80 http://www.amazon.co.uk/Brandtastic-Brand-Terrible-Sarah-Brummitt/dp/184426419X

81 http://www.amazon.co.uk/Silent-Messages-Implicit-Communication-Attitudes/dp/0534000592

83 http://www.gettyimages.co.uk/detail/news-photo/yasser-arafat-the-chairman-of-the-palestine-liberation-news-photo/1169719

84 http://news.bbcimg.co.uk/media/images/61202000/jpg/_61202872_ap9309130343.jpg

85 http://www.telegraph.co.uk/technology/bill-gates/10011847/Bill-Gates-disrespects-South-Korean-president-with-casual-handshake.html

86 http://www.theglobeandmail.com/news/world/in-photos-the-most-difficult-handshake-of-the-g20-meeting/article14125647/

87 http://www.telegraph.co.uk/news/worldnews/asia/china/11220368/Worlds-most-awkward-head-of-state-handshake-as-Xi-Jinping-and-Shinzo-Abe-meet.html

88 http://si.wsj.net/public/resources/images/OB-ZA520_0924sh_M_20130924112406.jpg

89 http://i.ytimg.com/vi/aFqxkZs4jG0/maxresdefault.jpg

90 http://www.telegraph.co.uk/news/worldnews/michelle-obama/6232298/Michelle-Obama-keeps-Silvio-Berlusconi-at-arms-length-at-G20.html

91 http://edition.cnn.com/2009/POLITICS/04/29/amanpour.obama.foreign.policy/index.html?eref=rss_world

97 http://citeseerx.ist.psu.edu/viewdoc/download?doi=10.1.1.407.1290&rep=rep1&type=pdf

82 http://www.amazon.co.uk/The-Definitive-Book-Body-Language/dp/0752858785

93 http://www.amazon.co.uk/What-Every-BODY-Saying-Speed-Reading/dp/0061438294

94   http://www.newstatesman.com/politics/2014/10/david-cameron-vs-ed-miliband-what-body-language-tells-us

95   http://www.telegraph.co.uk/news/politics/conservative/9592548/Conservative-Conference-sketch-David-Cameron-cleared-for-take-off.html

96   http://www.telegraph.co.uk/news/uknews/1567287/Scottish-question-leaves-Gordon-Brown-reeling.html

99   http://static.comicvine.com/uploads/ignore_jpg_scale_small/1/10268/320468-116953-wonder-woman.jpg

100   http://static.comicvine.com/uploads/original/11116/111164870/3847551-9865926659-batma.jpg

101   http://www.imdb.com/title/tt0800080/

102   http://healthland.time.com/2013/08/24/are-you-a-spreader-how-the-space-you-take-up-reveals-how-powerful-you-feel/

103   http://pss.sagepub.com/content/early/2013/09/25/0956797613492425

104   http://www.telegraph.co.uk/women/womens-life/11309866/Ban-manspreading-Brits-want-men-to-sit-with-their-legs-together.html

Chapter 7

3   The New Oxford Dictionary of English, Oxford University Press, 2001.

132   http://www.amazon.co.uk/Thinking-Fast-Slow-Daniel-Kahneman/dp/0141033576

133   http://www.theinvisiblegorilla.com/videos.html#tryit

134   http://www.druckerinstitute.com/peter-druckers-life-and-legacy/

135   http://www.amazon.co.uk/s/ref=nb_sb_noss_1?url=search-alias%3Daps&field-keywords=effective+executive

139   http://freakonomics.com

136   http://www.amazon.co.uk/Think-Like-Freak-Smarter-Everything/dp/1846147557

137   http://www.thefa.com/thefacup

138   http://www.snopes.com/college/homework/unsolvable.asp

140   http://www.smiletrain.org.uk

141   http://www.dailymail.co.uk/news/article-3081294/Britain-s-oldest-poppy-seller-dead-Avon-Gorge-aged-92.html

142   http://interruptions.net/literature/Jackson-JOSIT-01.pdf

54   http://www.mckinsey.com/insights/leading_in_the_21st_century/decoding_leadership_what_really_matters

36   http://www.daniellevitin.com/theorganizedmind/

55   http://www.mccombs.utexas.edu/departments/accounting/research/phd-reunion/~/media/82a1df43c311420892cfcf94ef48b8a9.ashx

56   http://www.alittlelab.stir.ac.uk/pubs/Quist_12_integratingsocial&physicalcues_JESP.pdf

57   http://courtroomlogic.com/2013/03/15/pitch-and-perception/

58   https://www.youtube.com/watch?v=RAJgnUix2kI

70   http://www.psychology.sdsu.edu/the-sound-of-power-how-a-position-of-power-can-change-your-voice/

59   http://www.woodyallen.com/

60   http://www.itv.com/news/london/2015-02-24/natalie-bennett-suffers-brain-fade-during-excruciating-interview/

61   http://www.amazon.co.uk/Pride-Prejudice-Wordsworth-Classics-Austen/dp/1853260002/ref=sr_1_1?s=books&ie=UTF8&qid=1430551773&

62   http://www.imdb.com/title/tt1723816/

63   http://www.bbc.co.uk/news/magazine-28708526

64   http://www.neighbours.com/

65   http://www.amazon.co.uk/Speak-Yourself-Impress-Influence-Impact/dp/0273785389

66   [http://dailymail.co.uk/sciencetech/article-2538554/want-promotion:Dont-speak-like-Aussie-Rising-pitch-end-sentences-make-sound-insecure.html]

67   http://www.amazon.co.uk/Oxford-Dictionary-Modern-Slang-Reference/dp/0199232059

68   http://www.bbc.co.uk/news/magazine-11426737

69   http://www.entrepreneur.com/article/243340

19   http://www.westwingepguide.com

41   http://www.newscientist.com/article/dn20848-the-secret-life-of-pronouns.html

42   http://www.metrolyrics.com/were-off-to-see-the-wizard-lyrics-wizard-of-oz.html

43   http://www.huffingtonpost.com/2014/12/08/persuasive-word_n_6276184.html

44   https://www.psychologytoday.com/blog/credit-and-blame-work/201201/mindlessness-work

48   http://www.goodreads.com/quotes/57583-being-powerful-is-like-being-a-lady-if-you-have

49   http://www.brainyquote.com/quotes/authors/a/arianna_huffington.html

Chapter 8

3   The New Oxford Dictionary of English, Oxford University Press, 2001.

106   http://www.huffingtonpost.com/2015/05/11/florence-seesee-rigney-90-year-old-nurse_n_7255190.html

107   http://www.theguardian.com/lifeandstyle/2012/feb/01/top-five-regrets-of-the-dying

143   http://www.ted.com/talks/larry_smith_why_you_will_fail_to_have_a_great_career?language=en

108   https://hbr.org/2015/04/5-signs-its-time-for-a-new-job

120   https://www.ted.com/talks/larry_smith_why_you_will_fail_to_have_a_great_career?language=en

151   https://www.youtube.com/watch?v=8zLx_JtcQVI

53   http://www.amazon.co.uk/Habits-Highly-Effective-People/dp/0684858398/ref=sr_1_1?s=books&ie=UTF8&qid=143003301 9&sr=1-1&keywords=7+habits+of+highly+effective+people

152   http://www.doyouremember.co.uk/memory/bunty

Chapter 9

3   The New Oxford Dictionary of English, Oxford University Press, 2001.

36   http://www.daniellevitin.com/theorganizedmind/

37   http://www.duarte.com/book/resonate/ AND
        http://www.duarte.com/book/slideology

38   https://news.virginia.edu/content/human-brains-are-hardwired-empathy-friendship-study-shows

39   http://www.innocentdrinks.co.uk/us/our-story

40   http://www.abrahamlincolnonline.org/lincoln/speeches/gettysburg.htm

45   http://www.amazon.co.uk/Rebecca-VMC-Book-Daphne-Maurier-ebook/dp/B0074ALZ7Q/ref=asap_bc?ie=UTF8

46   http://www.telegraph.co.uk/culture/culturepicturegalleries/9817505/30-great-opening-lines-in-literature.html?frame=2458291

76   http://www.amazon.com/The-Attention-Economy-Understanding-Currency/dp/1578518717

77   http://www.imdb.com/title/tt0098384/

78   http://changingminds.org/books/book_reviews/spin.htm

79   http://www.bbc.co.uk/programmes/b013pqnm

47   http://blog.ted.com/bill_gates_talk/